$ 2.25

SAUNDERS PHYSICAL ACTIVITIES SERIES

Edited by

MARYHELEN VANNIER, Ed.D.

Professor and Director, Women's Division,
Department of Health and Physical Education,
Southern Methodist University

and

HOLLIS F. FAIT, Ph.D.

Professor of Physical Education,
School of Physical Education,
University of Connecticut

TENNIS

second edition

ROBERT GENSEMER, Ph.D

Assistant Professor of Physical Education,
Department of Physical Education, University of Denver

ILLUSTRATED BY VIRGINIA FURBERSHAW

1975
W. B. SAUNDERS COMPANY • PHILADELPHIA • LONDON • TORONTO

W. B. Saunders Company: West Washington Square
Philadelphia, Pa 19105

12 Dyott Street
London, WC1A 1DB

833 Oxford Street
Toronto, Ontario M8Z 5T9, Canada

Library of Congress Cataloging in Publication Data

Gensemer, Robert E

Tennis.

(Saunders physical activities series)

Bibliography: p. 105

1. Tennis.   I. Title.

GV995.G4 1975   796.34'2   74–6682

ISBN 0–7216–4110–5

Saunders Physical Activities Series

Tennis   ISBN 0-7216-4110-5

Last digit is the print number: 9   8   7   6   5   4   3   2   1

Editors' Foreword

Every period of history, as well as every society, has its own profile. Our own world of the last third of the twentieth century is no different. Whenever we step back to look at ourselves, we can see excellences and failings, strengths and weaknesses, that are peculiarly ours.

One of our strengths as a nation is that we are a sports-loving people. Today more persons — and not just young people — are playing, watching, listening to, and reading about sports and games. Those who enjoy themselves most are the men and women who actually *play* the game: the "doers."

You are reading this book now for either of two very good reasons. First, you want to learn — whether in a class or on your own — how to play a sport well, and you need clear, easy-to-follow instructions to develop the special skills involved. If you want to be a successful player, this book will be of much help to you.

Second, you may already have developed skill in this activity, but want to improve your performance through assessing your weaknesses and correcting your errors. You want to develop further the skills you have now and to learn and perfect additional ones. You realize that you will enjoy the activity even more if you know more about it.

In either case, this book can contribute greatly to your success. It offers "lessons" from a real professional: from an outstandingly successful coach, teacher, or performer. All the authors in the *Saunders Physical Activities Series* are experts and widely recognized in their specialized fields. Some have been members or coaches of teams of national prominence and Olympic fame.

This book, like the others in our Series, has been written to make it easy for you to help yourself to learn. The author and the editors want you to become more self-motivated and to gain a greater understanding of, appreciation for, and proficiency in the exciting world of *movement*. All the activities described in this Series — sports, games, dance, body conditioning, and weight and figure control activities — require skillful, efficient movement. That's what physical activity is all about. Each book contains descriptions and helpful tips about the nature, value, and purpose of an activity, about the purchase and care of equipment, and about the fundamentals of each movement skill involved. These books also tell you about common errors and how to avoid making them, about ways in which you can improve your performance, and about game rules and strategy, scoring, and special techniques. Above all, they should tell you how to get the most pleasure and benefit from the time you spend.

Our purpose is to make you a successful *participant* in this age of sports activities. If you are successful, you will participate often – and this will give you countless hours of creative and recreative fun. At the same time, you will become more physically fit.

"Physical fitness" is more than just a passing fad or a slogan. It is a condition of your body which determines how effectively you can perform your daily work and play and how well you can meet unexpected demands on your strength, your physical skills, and your endurance. How fit you are depends largely on your participation in vigorous physical activity. Of course no one sports activity can provide the kind of total workout of the body required to achieve optimal fitness; but participation with vigor in any activity makes a significant contribution to this total. Consequently, the activity you will learn through reading this book can be extremely helpful to you in developing and maintaining physical fitness now and throughout the years to come.

These physiological benefits of physical activity are important beyond question. Still, the pure pleasure of participation in physical activity will probably provide your strongest motivation. The activities taught in this Series are *fun*, and they provide a most satisfying kind of recreation for your leisure hours. Also they offer you great personal satisfaction in achieving success in skillful performance – in the realization that you are able to control your body and its movement and to develop its power and beauty. Further, there can be a real sense of fulfillment in besting a skilled opponent or in exceeding a goal you have set for yourself. Even when you fall short of such triumphs, you can still find satisfaction in the effort you have made to meet a challenge. By participating in sports you can gain greater respect for yourself, for others, and for "the rules of the game." Your skills in leadership and fellowship will be sharpened and improved. Last, but hardly least, you will make new friends among others who enjoy sports activities, both as participants and as spectators.

We know you're going to enjoy this book. We hope that it – and the others in our Series – will make you a more skillful and more enthusiastic performer in all the activities you undertake.

Good luck!

MARYHELEN VANNIER

HOLLIS FAIT

Preface

This book is intended for anyone who plays tennis or is about to learn. Discussions of the skills of the game begin with fundamentals and progress to more refined analyses. This text is designed to offer something for everyone, but it is hoped that the details of the skills will not be overburdensome for the beginner nor too elementary for the intermediate or advanced player.

If you are a novice to the game, it is suggested that you first become familiar with the diagram showing facing page 1; then learn the rules presented in Chapter 4 and the terminology presented in the Glossary.

The explanatory descriptions of the skills are made from the standpoint of a right-handed player; consequently, if you are left-handed, you will need to transpose the narratives. Reference to the masculine gender throughout the text of course includes the ladies also.

The drawings in this text were based on photographs, and the author wishes to express his gratitude to The Macmillan Company for their permission to use the photographs of Lew Hoad, Rod Laver and Roy Emerson, and to Jerry Kalamen for taking the remaining pictures.

Contents

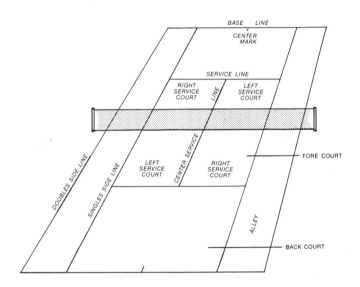

Diagram of a tennis court.

1

The Nature and Purpose of Tennis

When Don Budge was a young man he scorned tennis as a game of childish pursuit. Surely, he thought, no one with an adult mind could find stimulation in the simple act of batting a ball across a net only to have some other chap bat it back again, with insipid repetition of the whole affair. It was simple-minded animation engaged in by simple minds. Even marbles was less humdrum.

Eventually the reluctant Budge was persuaded by his brother to give tennis an honest trial, and his conception of the game subsequently underwent complete reversal. He became intrigued with the inexhaustible variety of playing methods and the enormous possibilities of tennis, and soon it captured all his spare moments. Ultimately Don Budge was to become the first man to win the coveted Gram Slam of tennis: the singles championships of the United States, England, France and Australia in the same year (1938), the most difficult and honored accomplishment in the world of tennis.

At this moment you probably do not view tennis with the same degree of apprehension that Budge once did, and it is also probable that you will not win the Grand Slam (although who really knows?). However slight or subtle, there is an interest in tennis on your part as evidenced by the fact that you have begun reading this book. If you do not know tennis you may want to learn it, or if you play a reasonable game you may want to improve it, or if you are very good you may want to be better. Whatever the reason, it's possible that you will come to a decision within the next several weeks as to the role the game will play in your active sports life. Even if you should decide that tennis is not for you, such a decision can intelligently and rationally be made only after you have given the game a fair trial.

Most likely you already know that tennis offers the participant every skilled and emotional involvement that is available in a non-contact sport. Tennis is first and foremost a game of genuine athletic skill, of that there is no question, but the wholesale production of strokes is not the complete test of the player. In many cases of com-

1

petition between players of equal skill, winners and losers are decided by factors other than raw skill. Of course, no one would deny
that an ability to stroke the ball effectively is an essential requisite
for continued success in tennis, but complementary to physical adroit-
ness is an acute mental approach to the game. No winning tennis
player ever laid his brain aside the court during a match. As with
the baseball pitcher and the football quarterback, each move of the
champion tennis player is based on a calculated risk, and as with the
players of billiards, thinking involves not only the play of the moment,
but the anticipated action several strokes ahead. Truly the mental involvement required of the tennis player equals that of any other sport.

In some respects, a tennis match is like a football game. You approach the contest with a planned strategy which invariably needs
alteration while the action is on because of the moves of your opponent. Then, like football, there is a pause between each attack allowing you time to inventory the success of your strategy and plan
new tactics.

Like most team sports but unlike most individual lifetime sports,
tennis requires stamina. The game makes a constant demand for
changes of direction with quick starts and stops. The outcome of many
a match has been determined by the strategy and durability of the
players. However, one of the noteworthy aspect of tennis is that the
pace of the game can be adapted to the participant's age. In fact, like
chess players, older players generally develop a seasoned sense of
gamesmanship which, in tennis, can offer effective compensation
for legs that no longer respond so vividly to the commands of the
mind.

Tennis is also a trial of an intangible quality called courage. There
never was, and there never will be, a tennis champion who doubted
his ability to play his best when circumstances demanded it. Every
champion had a ravenous appetite for victory which in itself could
not be satiated. The world of tennis is replete with stories of players
who burned the grass on the courts with their desire and fought for
comeback victories that would have made Frank Merriwell envious.

Tennis is like baseball in the respect that a clock does not determine the victor. Often you've seen a baseball team, hopelessly behind, begin a late inning rally, and someone would say, "The game
isn't over until the last man is out." A baseball team does not run out
of time, it runs out of outs. The tennis player, too, has the time he
needs to recover and try again and again for that comeback victory.
Score notwithstanding, if there is a point remaining to be played,
there is also time to claim your win, for the tennis match isn't over . . .
well, until it's over.

One of the great merits of tennis is that it has remained an au-
thentic game of sportsmanship despite its intensely competitive

nature. The final test of the player is the quality of his temperament. Universally inherent in this game are the player's hardy spirit of the contest and his good sportsmanship. Very rare, indeed, is the player who cheats in this game where dishonesty may affect the outcome. Perhaps it is because men and women of integrity are attracted to tennis, or maybe it's because tennis itself contributes a spirit of integrity. Whatever the source, an air of honorable sportsmanship surrounds the tennis courts. Those who compete demonstrate an overt respect for their opponents, and they win without boasting and lose without complaint.

Finally, the versatility of the game is such that both sexes can compete with and against each other, and tennis is played by peoples in every cultured country of the world. In the vernacular, the well-known inquiry of "Tennis, anyone?" could validly be paraphrased to "Tennis is for anyone."

The Background of Tennis and Its Great Players

The study of ancient cultures reveals some evidence that a form of tennis was played in the Greek and Roman Empires, and that a game in which a ball was batted back and forth with a type of racket may have been played in the Orient more than 2,000 years ago. Still other indications show that tennis began in Egypt and Persia 500 years before the Christian era.

Despite the obscurity of the ancient origins of tennis, there is no doubt that a tennis-like game was played in the parks and chateaus of thirteenth century France. Called by the name of *jeu de paume* (literally, game of the hand), it was first a bare-handed game of hitting a stuffed cloth bag over a rope. Rackets did not appear in use until the late fifteenth or early sixteenth century. As enthusiasm for the activity spread, larger towns, not having ample outdoor space, began building indoor courts in anything from cowsheds to monasteries. (In fact, monks were some of the earliest players.) It is this game, then, that is accurately referred to today as court tennis and is to be distinguished from the lawn tennis game (which was to become present-day tennis) that was not introduced until the nineteenth century.

Jeu de paume met with some unfavorable reactions in its early times, even to the point of being outlawed in a few areas, but the general popularity of the game continued on the climb. The growing acceptance did not wane even though King Louis X died in 1316 from a chill caught during a tennis match. Most of the fourteenth century French kings took up the sport, and the masses now found major recreation in it. And, by the close of the fourteenth century the game was well established in Holland and in England, where the writings of Chaucer indicate that it was called by its present name, tennis, although the origin of the word is subject to considerable controversy.

Following the historical pattern of so many other sports, monetary wagers on tennis matches soon became commonplace. Such practice encouraged professionalism, and by the beginning of the fifteenth century there were 1,400 professional players in France, even though the first written rules for the playing of tennis did not appear until 1599. In spite of the prevalence of gambling, tennis reached a peak of popularity in both England and France during the sixteenth and seventeenth centuries, Paris alone having built 1,800 courts. But the scandalous exchange of money almost obliterated the sport in the middle of the eighteenth century, and when the dust had settled from the French Revolution there was only one court remaining in use in Paris.

Civil war also depressed the playing of tennis in England, although the upper classes continued in their zeal for the sport. Then, in 1873, British Army Major Walter C. Wingfield introduced his guests at a garden party to a new outdoor game, incorporating many of the elements of court tennis but more similar to the present day game. Major Wingfield referred to the activity as "sphairistike," claiming it was the same game the ancient Greeks had played (sphairistike in Greek connotates "to play"). The English people were rapidly caught up with the game. Probably because it resembled court tennis played on a lawn, or maybe because no one could pronounce let alone spell the name, sphairistike soon became known as tennis-on-the-lawn, and eventually lawn tennis.

In attendance at the party when Major Wingfield introduced lawn tennis was an army officer who took the game with him to Bermuda as a diversion for the British garrison stationed there. Vacationing on the island during that winter of 1873-74, Miss Mary Outerbridge from New York became intrigued with the game. She learned to play it and brought some equipment with her when she returned to the United States. Customs officials debated a full week over what sort of duties should be levied on the strange-looking gear, then finally allowed it to enter tax-free.

As a family member of the Staten Island Cricket and Baseball Club, Miss Outerbridge received permission to lay out a court in an unused corner of the grounds. But the game found little favor with Club members. Women saw it as unladylike; they were too genteel to go chasing about after a little ball, and men were not willing to allow themselves to engage in an activity which included the word "love" as part of the scoring.

Despite this early rejection of tennis, within a few years it was included as an activity at nearly every major cricket club in the east, and soon its popularity would overstep its aristocratic boundaries to become a sport of the masses. But in these early years the rules for tennis were diverse, each club establishing its own regulations. This dissimilarity prompted an older brother of Miss Outerbridge to call a meeting of the leading cricket clubs at New York in 1881 for the purpose of standardizing the rules. An outcome of that meeting was the establishment of the United States Lawn Tennis Association (USLTA), still the ruling body of American tennis today.

Later that same year the first tournament for the National Championship of the United States was held at Newport, Rhode Island. Richard Sears won the title handily, and held it for the next six years, a record of consecutive championships still unmatched in any of the world's major tournaments. In 1915 the site for this great tournament became firmly established at the West Side Tennis Club in Forest Hills, Long Island, where it has been held annually (except in 1917) ever since.

The United States National Championship was not, however, the first important singles tournament. Four years earlier, in 1877, the English had inaugurated their National Championship at Wimbledon, a southwest suburb of London. Custom and tradition has since established the Wimbledon as the greatest tournament in the world. It is played today on grass courts which are manicured to perfection, and are generally considered the fastest anywhere. The British audience is knowledgeable, generous with their applause, and joined in presence by the queen and royal family, adding dignity to the general atmosphere that encourages the players to perform at their very best.

Spencer Gore won the first Wimbledon in 1877, taking full advantage of the fact that the net was 21 inches lower in the center than at the sides. He stationed himself just behind the net and repeatedly volleyed away his opponents' attempts at passing shots, but a year later the lob was devised, and Gore was easily overtaken. No one has ever considered Spencer Gore one of the all-time great players, but it is significant to note that even in those days tennis championships were won with the brain as well as the bat.

For a time the lob shot ended all net play, but in 1881 Bill Renshaw startled the Wimbledon crowds with a display of a daring smash shot to counteract the lob. No one had ever seen such play before, and his mastery of his skill earned Renshaw seven Wimbledon titles, six years consecutively, more than any player has since won.

In 1884, with the net down to its present day height, Wimbledon began an annual tournament for women, and three years later Lottie Dod, only fourteen years of age, became not only the youngest woman to win the Wimbledon, but the youngest player ever to win any major tournament. The tennis play of women in those early years was hindered by the modesty and formality of their attire, and by the fact that they all served underhand. However, these factors have changed dramatically, and public appreciation for women's tennis has grown rapidly.

When a British team was visiting the United States in 1900, Dwight F. Davis, then a student at Harvard, donated a trophy to be presented to the winner of a match between the team from England and an American team (of which Davis was himself a member). The trophy soon became known as the Davis Cup, and while it was originally intended to be awarded to the winner of an annual England-America match, it has grown today into the symbol of international team supremacy. It is believed that the competition for the Davis Cup, open to teams from all over the world, has done more to foster international good will than any other single sporting event.

Around the turn of the century the tennis world was stormed over by England's Doherty brothers. Reggie (Big Do) and Laurie (Little Do) are generally considered to have been the first all-court players, mastering every phase of the game. With their retirement the years prior to World War I were dominated by Sir Norman Brookes. The Australian lefty had an uncanny accuracy with all his shots, and was one of the greatest strategists the game has ever seen. American tennis during this time revolved around the California Comet, Maurice McLoughlin, who played a brawny attack game of serve and volley.

In the 20's tennis entered a golden era. William T. Tilden was to dominate the game as no one man had done before or since. He could play every type of spin from both his forehand and backhand, and his serve was referred to as the cannonball. All of this was coupled with his manificent physical stamina and his unbelievable dedication to the game. Often, for the sake of his fans, he would play right into an opponent's strengths just to demonstrate his superiority of skill. Those who saw him play are quick to agree that he may have been the greatest maestro of tennis skills the game has ever seen. And yet, were it not for Bill Tilden, the tennis world would look upon the 20's as the years of Little Bill Johnston. No match for Tilden, Bill Johnston was like a machine that never ran short of fuel, a constant show of determination that was an inspiration to other players. Although he played in the shadow of Tilden, the two of them together brought the attention of tennis to their native America.

The 20's also saw the game of the greatest woman player of all time, Suzanne Lenglen of France. A flamboyant personality both on the courts and off, she brought recognition to the ladies' game with her accurate placements and enthusiasm for the sport. Women's tennis received another boost when, in 1923, Hazel H. Wightman donated a cup to be awarded to the winner of a women's team match between England and the United States, an annual event between the two countries since that time. Mrs. Wightman was former American national champion herself, and the cup has appropriately become known as the Wightman Cup.

In the late 20's and early 30's the attention of the tennis world turned to France, where Henri Cochet, Rene Lacoste, and Jean Borotra, the French Musketeers, began a seven year reign as the game's best. Their dynasty was halted by the demolishing forehand drives of American Ellsworth Vines. Meanwhile, Helen Wills Moody, Little Miss Poker Face, enjoyed supremacy in women's tennis longer than any other woman before or since.

Fred Perry of England ruled the men's game for several years, but only until America's Don Budge backhanded his way to the Grand Slam. Then, in the 40's, Californian Jack Kramer showed the world of tennis what the big game was all about. Both his first and second serves simply screamed off his racket, and he would follow every one of them to the net to volley away the few weak returns his opponents would offer. Most modern players have adopted the Kramer attack style of tennis in these current days of the big game.

The 50's belonged to Pancho Gonzalez, an American. Some believe his serve was even more powerful than Kramer's, and many will contend that his all-court game was one of the best ever. In the female game, Little Mo, Maureen Connolly, was showing everyone that the ladies, too, could play the big game, which was first introduced in women's tennis by Alice Marble during the late 30's and early 40's. In the late 50's, American Althea Gibson became the dominant player in ladies' tennis.

Professional tennis, inaugurated in 1952, has often been a sometimes affair, but the pro organizations have usually bought up the best amateur players in the world each year. As a result, no one player has had a lengthy dominance in anateur tennis in recent times. However, in 1968, open tennis was approved for the first time, and now most of the world's great tournaments are available to amateur and professional players alike. Thus, the question of who is the best in the game no longer need be speculative, but can be settled on the courts. Additionally, the professional organizations have arranged world tours for their players, so that the best players are constantly competing against each other for prize money, adding further credence to answering the question of who is the most skilled.

Australian professionals Ken Rosewall, Lew Hoad, and Rod Laver, and American Arthur Ashe have generally been credited as the game's most prominent figures of the 1960's. In 1962 Laver became only the second player in history to win the Grand Slam, and immediately thereafter he turned professional. To show that his accomplishment was no accident, he repeated his performance in 1969 to become the first (and only) player to win the Grand Slam twice and the first to do it as a professional.

Laver has parlayed his talents into becoming the first to earn more than a million dollars in tournament prize money. He is unquestionably the number one player of modern times, and many a seasoned observer will contend that he may indeed be the best of any time to date.

No sport has ever gained in popularity as rapidly as tennis has in the 1970's. Public and private courts are overcrowded with racketeers of all ages and abilities. Indoor courts are booked a full season in advance even before they are constructed. Tennis camps and ranches are attracting clientele from all over the world. And television has shown the game to millions who were never before able to watch skilled levels of play. As a result, this augmented popularity of tennis has evolved far greater numbers of superb players than ever before. No longer do a handful of competitors dominate the game, as was true in years past. Nevertheless, some contemporary players can still be singled out. In the men's game there is the energetic and swift Tom Okker of the Netherlands, volatile Ilie Nastase from Rumania, Australia's power-hitter John Newcombe, and perhaps the best all-court player in the game today, Stan Smith of the United States. And of course, the 1970's cannot ignore the crashing serve of Ashe, the magnificent backhand of Rosewall, and the spinning accuracies of Laver.

It is the ladies' game, however, which has made the greatest advances in the 1970's. There is genuine interest in their play, prompted not only by their skilled performances, but also by their pulchritude. Australian Margaret Court must certainly be considered as one of the best players, on the basis of her long list of championships. The future "star" role will be played by the gifted young players, most notably Evonne Goolagong of Australia and America's Christ Evert. Still, it is Billie Jean King who is the most competitive player in the game today. She has not only demonstrated a mastery of on-the-court skills (and survived the bizarre challenge of Bobby Riggs), but has singularly campaigned for and effected a regard for the women's game. Largely through her efforts, most tournaments now pay equal prize money for men and women.

2

Needed Equipment and Its Care

Tennis equipment is relatively inexpensive and easy to transport. However, in choosing your equipment you should buy the very best you can, for the quality of your game will be somewhat dependent on the quality of your gear. Conscientious care will prolong the serviceability of your equipment.

Racket

The most important item of any player's equipment is the racket, and it is essential that you use discretion when buying it. Scrutinize the many available rackets carefully before deciding on the one that will be part of your game for at least the next several years. Swing them freely in the store, and have a ball with you to bounce off the strings (if, of course, they are already strung) so that your muscles will give you some pre-purchase impression of the feel of the bat in your hand.

The racket may be made of any material and in any conceivable size and shape. Technically, you could play the game with a baseball bat, a hockey stick, a frying pan, a fly swatter—anything. With this total lack of standardization it is quite surprising to find that rackets are produced with a uniform length of 27 inches and a face 9 inches across.

Recently the styles, materials, and playing qualities of rackets have proliferated to offer a tremendous choice to the buyer. Before 1930, all racket frames were a solid piece of wood. Today the wooden rackets are laminated strips (usually ash) synthetically bonded together under pressure and heat, and often interbonded with strips of maple, birch, bamboo, fiberglass, or spring steel. The grains of the wooden laminations (there may be anywhere from one to 11 laminations) oppose each other to prevent warping. There has been increased research into the effects of impact and vibration on the play-

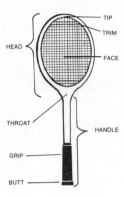

Parts of the racket.

ing ability of the racket. Refined bonding techniques have strength-
ened the rackets, and new innovations in design (such as open-
throated models) have made the current selection of wooden tennis
rackets far superior to former styles.

Metal and alloy rackets have enjoyed a great popularity recently,
and it is generally agreed that they are more resilient, and consequently livelier, than wooden rackets. This may be an advantage for
youngsters, some women, and older persons. However, wooden
rackets inherently have more effective ball-control characteristics, and
therefore should be the choice of beginners. Intermediate players
might wish the added power and flexibility of metal, or a wooden
racket bonded with metal. And finally, because of the over-all im-
provements in wooden models, it can no longer be concluded that
metal rackets are more durable than their wooden counterparts.

Ultimately, one must conclude that there is little comparative
information available. The best criterion is what one happens to
prefer, and what happens to feel comfortable. In short—to each his
own.

The circumference of the grip on all rackets will vary in 1/8 inch
intervals from 4⅜ to 5 inches. Some say the grip should allow you to
wrap your hand around it so that you can cover the nail of your third
finger with your thumb. Others believe the criterion for the proper
size is that there should be at least 1/2 inch between the tip of your
small finger and the heel of your hand. Still another gauge is when
your thumb, in a normal forehand grip, will come to the first knuckle
of your middle finger. Whatever your test, the grip should feel at
home in your hand. Be careful not to select a size which is so small
that it will turn from your hold when you stroke a firm shot. On the
better rackets the material of the grips themselves is perforated
leather with raised ridges. Plastic grips tend to slip in your grasp when
you perspire.

The weight of a racket is also important. A racket too light in weight will interrupt the smoothness of your swing resulting in jerky movements; a racket too heavy will make control and speed of the swing difficult. Weights range from 11½ to 15 ounces. Youngsters would do well to stay with the lighter weights, but adult women should try the 13 to 14 ounce range and men should consider at least 14 ounces. Of course, this is determined by your physique and therefore is a very individual matter. Proponents of a lighter racket say it increases one's "feel," and indeed the great Maureen Connolly used a racket of less than 13 ounces. However, most players and coaches agree that a heavier racket is the better choice in that it tends to aid the rhythm of the swing, a factor that is especially important for beginners. Keep in mind, though, that the racket you select you must still be able to control, and that a heavy bat does not automatically assure any player of a powerful stroke.

One additional factor concerning the weight: there is a difference as to how it is distributed. The balance point of most rackets (that point at which the racket would balance evenly on a knife edge) is 13½ inches from either end of a *strung* racket. An unstrung racket will balance heavier toward the butt end by 1/2 to 3/4 inch. Some players prefer a head-heavy racket, contending that it helps their base line game. Others believe the volley game is assisted by a handle-heavy racket. No experienced player will choose a racket that gives the feel of having its weight in the throat.

Rackets differ slightly in their over-all flexibility. Many players prefer a racket that is a bit more flexible to get the increased "snap" it imparts to the ball. Occasionally, you can find an article in one of the tennis magazines which will list the flexibility ratings of the more popular rackets.

Strings are of gut and nylon. Most top players string their rackets with gut. It is more resilient than nylon, giving the ball a bit more spirit as it jumps off the strings. In addition a ball hit off-center will still produce good results. However, gut frays quickly, especially if used in wet weather, and changes in humidity affect the tension of the stringing, occasionally even snapping a string or two. Total replacement is more frequent with gut, and never at a cost of less than ten dollars. Nylon, costing usually less than ten dollars for a stringing, will outlast gut and is immune to moisture and humidity changes. Therefore, it is more practical for the average player.

Strings are available in 15-, 16-, and 17-gauge thicknesses. Seventeen-gauge is the thinnest and least durable but the most resilient. Tournament players often use it, but the choice for most players is 15-gauge. The tension on the strings is spoken of in pounds per square inch, and can be controlled according to the player's wishes, gut generally being strung more tightly than nylon. Top players keep their rackets at 55 to 65 pounds, but the average player should use a 50 to 55 pound stringing. Former top-ranking amateur player Gardner Mulloy has suggested that beginners should use only a 40 pound tension. Taut stringing gives more life to a struck ball, but light stringing affords the player considerably more control, an important psychological advantage for beginners. Remember, too, that after half-a-dozen days of play on new strings they will have lost 2 or 3 pounds of their original tension.

Have your racket strung only by an expert, for faulty stringing may destroy the alignment of the frame. A solution of 50 per cent paint thinner and 50 per cent clear shellac will prolong the life of the strings, but use it only occasionally. Grips, too, should be replaced when worn. They are inexpensive, and a do-it-yourself job requires very little time. In dry climates leather grips need an occasional rubdown with a preservative. If most of your play is on hard surface courts a strip of adhesive tape across the tip of a woden racket will keep it from splintering when it touches the court in the normal course of play. A racket cover keeps moisture from the wood. In winter store wooden rackets in a press in a dry place.

Balls

Tennis balls are made of two cups of rubber molded together, covered with synthetic and wool felt, and inflated with compressed air or gas. Some will have an extra heavy covering of felt and are often labeled "heavy duty." Their play will outlast the "championship" balls, especially on hard surface courts. The quality of tennis balls is of much less concern to the player than is the quality of the racket. Specifications control the manufacture of balls, and those which have met the required standardizations will display a "USLTA Approved" stamp on the ball or package.

To maintain pressure most balls are packed in pressurized containers. They should be opened just before play, for once exposed the balls will lose their pressure fairly rapidly. Even in pressurized packing they may fall below the USLTA standard for pressure when stored six to eight months. Thus balls bought in the fall but not opened until the spring may have slightly less bounce than when they were packed. However, this problem has·been overcome by the new pressureless balls first produced in Sweden. This resiliency comes from the rubber itself rather than air pressure; pressurized packing is unnecessary. Many players like the fact that they often come four to a package instead of the usual three making the bother of ball-chasing on the courts less frequent. Others dislike the fact that they respond with a "heavy" feeling when struck. The covering of these balls is of wool-dacron, which will outlast others, but they have the disadvantage of tending to wear down the racket strings faster than other balls.

Brightly colored balls have exploded across the tennis scene, replacing the white ones in popularity. Even the USLTA no longer decrees that, for tournaments, "the ball shall be white in color." Yellow or orange tennis balls are more reflective, and consequently are easier to follow against distracting backgrounds. However, in controlled testing, other colors (notably red) have not proven to be more easily visible than white.

Tennis balls will last for three to ten sets, depending on the experience of the players and the court surface. Concrete is especially punishing to tennis balls. Dampness and extreme temperatures are also enemies to the life of the balls, and balls should be stored in cool, dry areas.

When the bounce is gone from old balls they should be discarded. If they will not bounce back to at least the height of your knees when dropped from the shoulder, then their life is gone. And, the loss of their nap also means they should be thrown away. Beginners who insist on using skinned balls that are "good to the last bounce" will find themselves adapting their swing to the ball and consequently developing habits not consistent with sound tennis. However, if the balls are still lively but have lost a bit of their nap, they can be revitalized by putting them in the family washer. They will look and play like new when they're dry.

Clothing

Gone is the traditional humdrum all-white tennis attire that dominated the sports for decades. It has yielded to tinted shirts, vivid skirts, and hued shoes. The influx of colors and new designs for both men and women is a sign that the apparel of tennis is keeping pace with the expansion of the game. In fact, in the opinion of many, the spirited fashion revolution has in itself helped the growth of tennis. Instead of the prosaic white uniform, all kinds of colors and designs are now acceptable and commonplace.

It remains functional, however, for men to wear knit shirts and shorts which are cut especially for tennis. Women may chose a tennis dress, a shorts-and-shirts outfit, a jump suit, or any of the pleated, knitted, ribbed, buttoned, racing-striped, multi-colored trousseaus. About the only precaution for women is to avoid those overly ruffled raiments and overbearingly feminine designs. Generally, women players (and men, to a lesser degree, because of a more limited choice), can develop a wardrobe of matching mixables and classy colors to compliment their personage and the game.

Tennis fashion has also grown to include modish warm-up suits which are very utilitarian. Sweaters and light jackets are also attractive. For footwear, it is best to choose a top-of-the-line shoe that combines playing durability with comfort. Flat soles are essential if the court is not hard-surfaced; otherwise the court will be damaged.

Men often wear a sun shade or floppy hat. Women can experiment with hats, barrettes, elastic bands, and scarves to keep hair in place. Some women choose to wear a tennis glove to save their hand from callouses. Many players will wear a wrist band on their hitting arm to keep perspiration from the handle of their racket.

In conclusion, the total tennis outfit is one's personal choice. The only advice is to avoid overspending the budget.

3

Basic Skills

If you can throw a ball, swat a fly, run and walk, you can learn to play tennis. Tennis involves basically the skills of running and throwing. Speed of foot is certainly a valuable requisite to the tennis player, but this is essentially an innate quality that cannot be significantly altered. Therefore tennis techniques must be concerned with the second of the two skills: that of throwing. But before you attend to any of the details of the throwing motions, you must first create the proper muscular attitude for learning.

Getting the Feel of the Ball

First use your racket to dribble the ball as you would a basketball, then tap it lightly into the air, and try a combination of both, keeping the ball alive for a while. Notice how the ball reacts, and how you must hold the racket to control it. Have a friend toss some balls to you and hit them back. Then drop the ball and stroke it across the net from the bounce. Finally you and your friend should hit freely back and forth from opposite sides of the net. Hit those balls which come to your left side as well as those to your right. Tap a few, punch some others, and take a hardy swing at the rest. Notice the response of the ball each time you stroke it; how hard you must swing to have it cross the net and how controlled your swing must be to keep it in the court. Change the angle of your racket face and note the difference in the resulting ball flight. And toss some balls just over your head to stroke in the fashion of the serve.

In this first active contact with tennis your objective is to let your mind and muscles receive and record the impressions of hitting the ball. This incorporates perceptions and sensations different from hitting a baseball or a golf ball or a badminton shuttlecock or anything else.

Excluding the serve, perhaps ninety per cent of your strokes will be made on a ball that has bounced. As your skill increases, you'll take more balls from flight before the bounce, but for now your game will revolve around what are known as the ground strokes: the forehand and backhand. Even as a highly skilled player these strokes will remain as your staple game. They are the backbone of defense, and when all else fails, they will normally keep your game alive.

Swing the racket head in a fluid motion in a free and easy sweep from start to finish. In the forehand this resembles throwing a baseball sidearm; the backhand is like throwing a Frisbee but with a firm wrist. To get the feel of the swing, hold the racket near the butt and swing it rhythmically, using a free-play arm motion that moves the racket head smoothly across your body and into and through the ball. Try swinging with your eyes closed to further the feeling of a relaxed, rhythmic swing.

Grip

THE EASTERN GRIP. *Have someone extend a racket to you with the face exactly perpendicular. Clutch the handle of the racket as you would the hand of a friend. Your palm will be in the same plane as the racket face, and the heel of your hand rests against the butt. Spread your fingers as much as possible without being uncomfortable, and extend your index finger into a "trigger finger" formation under the handle. Your thumb will wrap around the handle to make contact with or lie adjacent to the inside of your middle finger.* Notice in the illustration that the index finger is spread considerably more than the others to form the "trigger finger." It is imperative that the thumb wrap around the handle rather than resting on top where it would destroy the leverage of the grip. The knuckle in your index finger nearest the palm is placed *exactly in back of the handle.* In this proper position *the bulk of your hand is in back of the handle,* and the racket face becomes an extension of your palm. Make sure that the butt of the handle does not rest inside the heel of your hand, but instead extends slightly beyond the heel toward you. Although you may find it a bit unnatural to spread your fingers, you will need them in this position to gain the full lever advantage that this grip affords.

The Eastern Backhand Grip. This grip involves a change from the forehand of a quarter turn (of a full circle) counterclockwise to your left. *To attain the eastern backhand grip, have someone extend a racket to you, again with the face perpendicular. Lay your palm on top of the handle with your wrist slightly to the left. Spread your fingers comfortably as you wrap them around the handle, again extending your index finger. Place your thumb at a 45 degree diagonal across the back of the handle, not in contact with any of your fingers. The knuckle in your index finger nearest the palm rests on top of the*

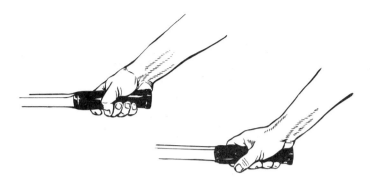

The eastern grip.

handle, slightly to the right. There is some disagreement among top players as to the correct position of the thumb in the eastern backhand grip. Most suggest that it should be kept at a diagonal, but some assert that better leverage is attained if it is run straight up the handle toward the head of the racket. This is an individual matter of comfort, but women may well try the thumb straight up the handle for the additional support it tends to give the backhand. Some men, too, may find that this position acts as a sort of brace against the impact of the ball in the backhand drive, but there is an inclination for the shot to be pushed rather than stroked when the thumb is parallel with the handle. If your wrists are strong, the diagonal position across the back of the handle is recommended. In any case, the eastern backhand finds *the bulk of your hand on top of the handle,* and the butt extending slightly beyond the heel of your hand.

THE WESTERN GRIP. This grip, now obsolete, originally became popular for play on hard surface courts where the ball takes a high bounce. The grip lends itself to high stroking, and top spin is readily imparted to the ball with the western. The western backhand grip is basically that of the eastern, but the forehand constitutes quite a difference. To feel the grip of the western forehand simply lay the racket on the court then pick it up by the handle. Your hand will be about a quarter turn to the right of the eastern forehand. You can now see that hitting low shots would be difficult, and that a considerable shift of the hand would be necessary for the backhand.

THE CONTINENTAL GRIP. A third way to hold the racket is in a grip that is midway between the eastern forehand and backhand, called the *continental.* It offers a distinct advantage in that *no change is made from the forehand to the backhand,* and thus has become popular among net players whose exchange of shots is so rapid that

The continental grip.

shifting the hand is difficult. Some instructors advocate the continental grip for beginners to avoid the confusion of shifting the hand. Sometimes called the hammer grip, it requires a strong wrist and sound stroking ability. It is not effective for a powerful forehand drive, but the ball can be taken on the rise more easily, an advantage when charging the net. *For the continental grip, move your hand slightly to the left from the eastern forehand. The palm rests somewhat on top of the handle, and the knuckle nearest the palm in your index finger is on the bevel of the handle. Maintain the same spread of the fingers and lay of the thumb that you do in the eastern forehand.*

The mechanics of the eastern and the continental grips are basically the same. You may want to test the comfort of both grips, but you should be fully aware of the contemporary beliefs among top players and coaches as to the most economical use of the grips. *Very few recommend exclusive use of either the eastern or the continental grip for ground stroke play. Instead, experienced players use the eastern grip for the forehand and the continental grip for the backhand. In the backhand there may be a very slight rotation from the classic continental toward the classic eastern grip, but almost all experienced players do employ the eastern forehand and a continental backhand.* Within this context, it is probably well for even beginning players to utilize these two grips for the ground strokes. At the risk of redundancy, it should be repeated: *the most mechanically advantageous use of the grips is to play an eastern grip for forehand shots, and a continental grip (with perhaps a very slight turn toward the eastern backhand) for backhand shots.* Eventually, you will find that these grips settle your hand on the racket with a sense of belonging, and that your swing will be comfortable and your shots accurate.

The Ground Strokes

THE READY POSITION.   The efficiency of the forehand and backhand drives (or of any of the other strokes, for that matter) is partially dependent on what the player does prior to the actual hitting action.

The Ready Position

Effective stroking really begins (and ends) with a basic position of readiness that prepares the player to move in any direction for the return of his opponent's shots. The player who does not assume the basic ready position will find himself frequently being rushed into pressing his strokes; that is, hitting with too short a backswing, or hitting while off-balance.

The ready position is essentially the same whether one is at the net, playing the base line, or awaiting a serve. It is uncomplicated, but it must become ingrained as the habitual between-stroke stance. In many ways the position resembles that of a baseball shortstop: *feet comfortably spread about shoulder width, knees flexed but under no strain, back fairly straight and inclined forward, head up, and eyes on the opponent. Do not actually lean forward, but keep your weight on your toes. Face your opponent and point your racket toward him (without stretching out your arms) so that you can draw it as easily into either the forehand or the backhand. (Avoid the common tendency of holding the racket across your body rather than extending it toward your rival.) Cradle the throat of the racket in your left hand, keeping its head higher than the handle, and hold the racket with a relaxed forehand grip. Keep all of the muscles of your body in a state of readiness.*

FUNDAMENTALS OF THE GROUND STROKES.   By now you should
have your muscles programmed to swing the racket in the free and
fluid sweeping motion that is so important for consistent stroking.
Your tennis practice should give you a rhythmical swing that is unhindered by the details of the strokes. As a novice, you must learn
to resist the apparently overwhelming temptation common to beginners to pat the ball across the net rather than stroking it freely. This af-
finity for tapping the ball originates from two sources. One is mechanical and will take up our discussion for the next few pages. The
other is the natural desire of a beginning player to be successful, thus
to keep the ball in-bounds by steering it over the net instead of risking
a full swing. Such a pat-ball approach may win you plenty of back-yard
badminton games and probably even a few tennis matches (as long as
you compete against other beginners), but it will be rather embar-
rassing if you try it against a skilled opponent. To learn the strokes of
tennis you must avoid pat-ball jabs at the ball and swing freely in
order to hit it, regardless of how negative the early results may be.

THE FOREHAND DRIVE.   This is the most frequently used stroke
in tennis (excluding possibly the serve) and often is a player's strongest asset. Although it may be difficult to play a respectable game
without a backhand, it is almost impossible without a forehand.

Most players feel the forehand is the easiest stroke to learn because it is a natural movement. In many ways it resembles the action
of a baseball batter. To feel this resemblance, take a batting stance
(a slightly opened stance) just in front of the base line and have someone stand near the net to act as a pitcher. Hold the racket in one hand
with a forehand grip, at waist level, and pointed directly away from
the net. Have the "pitcher" toss some balls to you so that they *bounce*
into your strike zone. Without taking a step, hit the balls across the
net. After a dozen or more successful hits, take a step with your left
foot toward the net as you hit, shifting your weight onto that foot as
the baseball batter does. Baseball players refer to this as "stepping
into the ball," and teachers of tennis often tell their students to do the
same, but in reality *your step must not be toward the ball, but toward
the net.*

When you have grasped the idea of stepping toward the net as
you swing, then assume the ready position after each hit and pivot
from it into the batting stance as the ball is on its way. Do not worry
about any footwork in the pivot—just get quickly into the batting
stance.

It is during this change from the ready position to the hitting position that many beginners lose a basic and important fundamental.
*As you pivot from the ready stance you must get into a hitting posi-
tion that finds your feet, hips and shoulders all facing the right side
line. Often the novice will fail to make this complete pivot. Unless*

you turn from the ready position to face the side line before you swing, you will not be able to draw the racket into a complete back- swing, and as a result you will find yourself punching at the ball rather than taking a clean swing.

Begin to take the racket into the backswing with *both* hands, then let your left hand come off the throat quite naturally on the way back. Finally, finish off your stroke with a follow-through that carries the racket in front of your left shoulder, arm fairly straight all the way. This entire maneuver, from the ready position to the follow-through, somewhat resembles that of a baseball infielder who has taken a ground ball and thrown it sidearm to first base.

THE BACKHAND DRIVE. In its most elementary form, the back- hand involves the same mechanics as the forehand, but is performed on the opposite side of your body. Learn it the same way as the fore- hand by taking a left-handed batting stance, pointing the racket away from the net, and first swinging without the stride; then incorporate the step into your swing and finally pivot from the ready position into the backhand hitting position. The one distinctive difference of the backhand hitting position from the forehand is in the shoulder pivot. *The shoulders must be turned more than they are for the forehand.*

The backhand drive.

They make more than a 90 degree turn (from the ready position) so that with the completion of the backswing you are looking over your right shoulder to see the approaching ball. As in the forehand, your stroke should be completed in a follow-throw that finishes with the racket extended in front of your right shoulder.

Consider now the importance of the weight shift during the stroke. It is the same principle as employed by the boxer who steps toward his adversary when throwing a punch to gain the full thrust of his blow. This forward push from off his back foot generates the boxer's power, for it starts the force of his momentum toward his target. The baseball batter does the same, shifting his weight forward so that at the moment of contact with the ball his weight is largely on the front foot. If you have ever carefully watched someone putting the shot you know that at the moment of release the weight is also on the forward foot. Even a golfer presses his weight toward the target at the moment of contact, although he does not take a step. In fact, in every sport where explosive power is important, the generation of that power is a total body movement that includes a shift in weight toward the target.

Now, tennis does not demand that you hit each shot with maximum effort, but if you were to swing the racket while standing flat-footed, the power for the stroke would need to come mainly from your arm, and therefore control of the swing would be more difficult. *The forehand and backhand strokes are mechanically more efficient when your weight is moving toward the net and on the forward foot when the ball is contacted. The swing involves your entire body, not just your arm alone.*

These few principles form the basis of the ground strokes. When you can execute a fluid swing within these guidelines, you will hit a ball effectively regardless of its bounce or approaching speed, or your position on the court.

Details of the Forehand Drive. Next, add some polish to your forehand to make it a lethal offensive weapon. Consider first of all the backswing. A large, looping backswing is no longer popular, not even among the experienced professional players. *The length of the backswing is primarily determined by how hard you want to stroke the ball, but even when you want to hit a ball full-out, the racket should not be forced into an exaggerated backswing. Always stop the backswing when you feel the muscles of your arm begin to tighten.* If you are accustomed to a big backswing, practice a shorter one for those emergencies when the speed of the approaching ball does not allow you to take your normal swing.

The backswing is an arc, but not similar to the swinging of a gate to which it is often likened. No effort should be made to keep the racket parallel to the ground in the manner of a "flat" swing. *The head of the racket becomes raised on its trip back so that at the completion of the backswing it is higher than the handle.* A few top players even finish their backswing with the racket pointing directly skyward.

At the end of your backswing your weight has settled quite naturally on your rear foot, ready to push off toward the net, but never "rock" your weight back as you take your backswing.

Re-emphasis here needs to be given to the shoulder turn. Remember that in the finish of the backswing, the shoulders and the hips both must *face toward the right side line.* Only from this position can you get the racket back to execute a free-wheeling forehand drive. If this pivot of the shoulders and hips remains a problem for you, practice drawing the racket back while keeping your left hand on the throat as long as possible, thus forcing your shoulders to turn.

One thing that is unforgivable in the backswing is leading the motion with your elbow. Actually, in contrast to what many people believe, the only part of the hitting arm (which includes the racket as an extension of your arm) that travels parallel to the court in the backswing is your elbow. *Throughout the backswing and into the foreswing up to the moment of contact with the ball your elbow must remain low and fairly close to your body. If your elbow leads the arm in the backswing the racket head will "drag," a factor that will destroy the timing of the swing and slow it down considerably.* This is especially a hazard when playing on fast hard-surface courts where the ball skips instead of bounces. If you find yourself consistently hitting late on your forehand drives, or if you feel like you never have enough time to make a firm stroke, you are lifting your elbow and leading it in the backswing. Golfers call this a "flying elbow," and they have an old trick for curing it that works as well with tennis players. Simply take a tennis ball and tuck it under the hollow of your right arm at the shoulder. If the ball drops to the court when hitting a normal forehand, then your elbow is flying. All good players keep their elbow down throughout the backswing. Pancho Gonzales, for example, pointed his racket straight up at the finish of the backswing. So did Don Budge. But they kept their elbow parallel to the court as they took the racket back. It is the only way to execute a smooth swing.

There are, however, a few times when it is impossible to keep your elbow down, such as when you must hit a high bounding ball. Otherwise, the elbow must be kept from flying.

As you prepare to bring the racket into the ball, begin a step toward the net just prior to your foreswing. Notice again, the step is *toward the net* and not toward the ball. Unless you have had a hard run for the ball and you cannot do otherwise, *never step across your body with your forward foot. If you do, it will put your left side in the way of your forward swinging arm and will thus work against your own power. Your left side, at the moment of contact, must be pulled around toward the net to allow your hitting arm to come through unhindered.* To use an example from golf again, they call this problem "blocking out with the left side," and a golfer can rectify it by starting his forward swing with the hips and shoulders instead of the arms. Tennis players must do the same. As soon as you take your forward step, pull your shoulders and hips around toward the net, assisting the pivot with a bit of a thrust from your left arm. By the time contact is made, your shoulders and hips are almost in a position parallel with the net.

The racket and your weight will have come forward together, so that at the moment of contact your weight is on your forward foot and the heel of your rear foot is raised. As in the backswing, your elbow travels parallel to the court. *At contact your wrist must be firm, almost locked with your forearm, to insure the full utilization of your hitting power.*

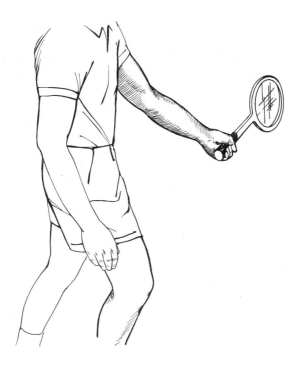

Consider now a fundamental principle of physics that is important in the action of the wrist and the path of the forearm. According to the law of rebound, a struck tennis ball will travel essentially in the direction the racket head was traveling at the moment of contact. Therefore, the longer the racket head is moving in the direction you want to hit the ball, the more likely it is that the ball will be accurately placed. All this is accomplished quite normally in the proper swing, for while the forehand drive carries the racket through an arc, that arc tends to flatten out as the racket approaches the ball. This flattening is in turn the result of two factors, the first of which is the action of the arm. *In the completed backswing the elbow is somewhat flexed, but as the racket comes into the ball the elbow unbends and extends, giving the foreswing a hint of a pushing motion. This action is coupled with a wrist that is firm and laid back (cocked) at contact. The elbow trails the wrist when the ball is met, the butt of the racket is near the front surface of your body, and the ball is thus contacted not alongside your body but out in front. The whole secret to the motion is a laid-back wrist at contact, and the secret to the laid-back wrist is to cock it into that position during the backswing.* While the racket is being taken back the wrist begins to cock, so that at the finish of the backswing the wrist has already been laid back. In the foreswing, then, the wrist remains steady, without the snapping motion that is used in throwing a ball. A study of the sequential sketches of the forehand on pages 24 to 26 will show that the wrist and racket are already laid back at the start of the foreswing and remain in that position up to the time of contact. This cocked wrist will quite naturally give you an unbending of your elbow for an "inside-out" foreswing that flattens the arc of the racket head and allows your arm and racket to travel in the same forward motion for a brief moment. It is, then, a bit of a "pushing" swing, and will provide you with the feeling of "hitting through the ball" that all tennis teachers impress upon their students.

It must be recognized that, if you have chosen to use the continental grip instead of the eastern forehand, the laid-back wrist will not be cocked quite so far, and the ball must be met more alongside of your body.

After contact, the natural motion of the arm is to roll the racket and wrist to the left, and this should complete your swing. However, this must be the motion only *after* the ball has been sent on its way, for if you begin to roll the wrist before contact you will close the racket face (turn it toward the ground) and hit the ball into the net. To avoid this rolling motion, contact the ball with your elbow still slightly flexed rather than locked in a fully extended position. Remember that after you have hit the ball there is no effort to stop the momentum of the racket by "pulling up" with your arm. Let the racket come to rest naturally, and regain your ready position for the next stroke.

Details of the Backhand Drive. For many players the backhand is a defensive stroke rather than an attacking weapon. Those who lack confidence in their backhand often merely pat the ball instead of risking a full swing, or run around their left side to use their more reliable forehand. The importance of mastering the backhand is that most opponents will attack that side, and if they find it to be weak, they will often use a drive to the left flank as an opportunity to move into the more advantageous net position.

To play tennis well, you need to include the backhand in your arsenal, but be perfectly willing to accept the fact that its development may be slower than the forehand. Those players who already have a strong backhand have invariably spent a great deal of time practicing it. The great Bill Tilden, who had mastered both the backhand and forehand equally well, once passed up all tournament play for a full year just to concentrate on perfecting his backhand. Most people believe the stroke is infinitely more difficult to learn than the forehand, while others will contend that it should be easier since the racket is swung away from instead of into the body. Regardless, you will find that when you improve your backhand, your forehand will seem easier and more fluid.

Many youngsters who feel they do not have the strength to hit a firm backhand will subconsciously start swinging the racket with both hands in an effort to add power to their stroke. In reality it is usually a too-heavy racket that hinders them rather than a lack of strength. Even some top players (Cliff Drysdale and Chris Evert are prime examples) have made effective use of the two-handed shot. This is not to say that beginning players should learn to hit two-handed, but there is little doubt that the left hand is more active in the backhand than it is in the forehand. *From the ready position, it is the left hand (already cradled around the throat of the racket) that does the work of pulling the racket into the backswing, while at the same time turning it for the backhand grip.* The motion begins with the left hand *lifting* the racket slightly and giving it a neat little twist so that you can adjust to the backhand grip, and then pulling the racket around into the completed backswing. At the start of the foreswing the left hand will naturally come off the racket, although there are some who teach that it should first *push* the racket into the foreswing.

This use of the left hand to pull the racket into the completed backswing will bring your shoulders and hips into their proper pivot. Remember again that *the shoulders and hips pivot more for the backhand than they do for the forehand.* At the end of the backswing you will be looking over your right shoulder at the ball.

As in the forehand, *your elbow remains close to your body throughout the backswing, traveling in a path fairly parallel to the court.* Get relatively close to the ball (without feeling cramped) as you bring the racket back.

The face of your racket, resting perpendicular to the court in the ready position, changes its angle quite normally on its trip into the backswing to finish somewhere between the vertical and the horizontal. (No effort should be made to keep the racket head "standing on edge" in the backswing.) The head of the racket will complete the backswing higher than the handle. Do not point the racket straight up in the air, however; if you do you will lose speed and power in the foreswing.

The foreswing starts with a turning of the hips and shoulders toward the net, arm and racket trailing. Many beginners have a tendency to push out at the ball with their elbow leading rather than starting the swing with the hips and shoulders, a disastrous fault. If you find a leading elbow to be one of your problems, have a friend hold the tip of your racket (with the racket in the position it would be at the end of the backswing), then use a shoulder pivot only (not your arm) to pull it from his grasp. This should give you the idea of trailing your arm and a feeling of power for the foreswing.

Your elbow and racket start the foreswing in close to your body, then travel on a path forward and away from your body. Your wrist and elbow will extend naturally to reach out for the ball so that *at*

impact your arm is extended but never locked. The ball is met with
the racket and your forearm in the same vertical plane, that is, neither
your elbow, wrist nor the racket head is leading. To insure maximum
control and power in the stroke, the head of the racket must be
slightly higher than the handle on contact, with the wrist firm and
your hand in a vise-tight grip. Since the racket is braced by your
thumb only instead of the palm and all fingers as it is in the forehand,
it is particularly important to keep the wrist and grip firm on impact.
The straightening of your arm as you come into the ball should give
you a feeling that power is being released and that the racket head is
accelerating at contact.

Step into your stroke just as you do for the forehand, weight on
the forward foot when the ball is met. However, in contrast to the

footwork of the forehand, *it is recommended that the step into the backhand drive be taken somewhat across your body.* By so doing you can make a longer backswing. A shortened backswing, usually a common feature of a beginner's backhand stroke, will deprive you of power.

It is imperative that your forward knee be flexed when the ball is hit. Although the forward knee should be flexed for both ground strokes, it is especially important in the backhand, otherwise your power will not flow into the ball, and instead you will have a tendency to lean back on the stroke, usually resulting in a ball hit out-of-bounds beyond your opponent's base line. This tendency to lean back on the backhand drive appears to be very common for inexperienced players. It results in lifting the right shoulder, bringing the elbow up too high. To prevent this, you should keep your shoulders parallel to the court throughout the swing, your elbow close to your body and travelling horizontally in the foreswing, and you should shift your weight onto the forward foot at impact.

Finish off the stroke with a clean follow-through, racket coming to rest high in front of your shoulder. After contact there is a natural tendency for your wrist to roll slightly, but as in the forehand, if this wrist roll occurs too soon the racket face will close and the ball will be netted.

THE USE OF THE GROUND STROKES IN MATCH PLAY. This discussion of the ground strokes so far is based on the assumption that the ball, during a match, will always float lazily up to you in a perfect hitting position. But, of course, any resourceful opponent will not let that happen. If you were always given adequate time to produce your strokes, the copybook fashion would be the most effective, but the pace of the match generally forces you into making alterations of your stroking techniques, sometimes even violating basic principles.

Your opponent will try to keep you on the move, and this will require that you repeatedly come quickly out of the ready position and into a run to retrieve his placements. This demands an explosive start. To discover the best way to get that start for hitting a ball on either side, get in the ready tennis position. This is very similar to the stance of a baseball base runner on first base who is about to attempt a steal of second. The runner can generate his greatest acceleration by pushing off with his left foot while at the same time taking a *short* step toward second base with his right, toes pointed in that direction, followed by a cross-over step with his left foot. The tennis player should use this same technique. *To achieve a quick start from the ready position, push off the foot opposite the side the ball is on (i.e., push off the left foot to move for a ball to your right), while at the same time taking a short step with your other foot in the direction of the spot on the court where you believe you will intercept the ball, toes pointed in that direction. Then follow with the cross-over step.*

Turn your shoulders into the direction of your run, but keep your head toward the approaching ball so that you may have a full binocular view of its flight.

Now for the most important feature of this run: you must draw the racket back into hitting position during *the run, not when you reach the ball. Getting the racket back slowly constitutes a major common fault among inexperienced players. If you hesitate in this respect your backswing will need to be rushed and your only recourse will be to return the ball down-the-line (parallel with the side line) and never cross-court.* It should be pointed out, however, that the backswing should normally be abbreviated (but never rushed) when you are forced to hit a forehand or backhand on the run.

As you approach the spot where you will intercept the ball, your run changes to a shuffle and you "soft shoe" your way into the proper hitting position. When time allows, take your step toward the net as you hit, then quickly recover your balance for the next stroke. However, when you do not have time to get into a hitting position, all techniques of stroking must be thrown out the window. *When you reach the ball while on a dead run, or when the ball is upon you before you have time to set yourself for the return, pay no mind at all to your footwork, and so on. Just use all your efforts to get your racket on the ball.* Study the sketch of the player on this page. In this instance he is receiving a wicked, slicing serve, and is returning

A step cannot be taken toward the net as the ball is contacted in this position.

the ball with his weight falling backward and on the "wrong" foot, but in this case there is no "wrong" technique. In fact, there is no technique at all save that of putting the racket to the ball in any way possible.

Another condition of match play that will innovate your swing is that you will not be able to hit every ball at the ideal waist height. *Generally, the racket should be taken into the backswing at about the height you will meet the ball.* However, regardless of the height of your swing, you must always try to maintain the same relative angle between your forearm and racket that you would use for a belt-high ball. This includes attempting to keep the racket head higher than your wrist at impact. Understandably, this is difficult to do when you are forced to hit a very low bounding ball. To keep the racket head up you must bend your knees, sometimes even bringing the back knee almost to the court, and lean over to get down to the ball (see sketches on page 36 and turn back again to the sketch on page 34).

In order to vary the placements of your shots, you must vary the place you contact the ball in the arc of your swing. To borrow again from baseball for illustration, when a right-handed batter wants to pull a ball to left field he must meet the ball out in front of the plate, and when he wants to punch a ball to right field he must delay his swing and hit the ball back further (closer to the catcher). The same technique must be used by the tennis player. *Placing the ball is a matter of timing the swing, not of changing the swing. To place a ball to your left you must meet the ball early, out in front of your body, and to hit a ball to your right you must delay the swing to hit the ball later, more alongside of your body.* Hitting to the right also includes delaying the weight transfer so that at contact some weight remains on your rear foot, while in hitting to the left all your weight will have come off the rear foot. Hitting to the left is somewhat easier since the racket head has more time to gain speed; when placing the ball to the right you will need to hit more firmly to impart the same velocity to the ball.

There is considerable disagreement among players and teachers as to exactly when in its bounce the ball should be met. It could be hit as it is rising, at the peak height of its bounce, or as it is descending, and there are arguments for each. Taking the ball on the rise will give your opponent less time to recover from his shot and he may therefore have one side of his court unguarded. Also, you will need to supply less of your own power for your stroke since the ball will, when rising, have its greatest speed. At the peak of its bounce the ball is traveling its slowest since it has lost the power of its ascent and gravity still has not drawn it downward. Therefore, proper timing of the swing should be facilitated when taking the ball at its highest point since it sort of "sits" up there waiting to be hit. In addition, the higher the ball is when it is hit, the "lower" the net will be, and consequently

more court space is available for the placement. Finally, taking the ball on the descent will bring the racket squarely into the ball since most players have a natural tendency to swing slightly upward, and it will allow you more time to get set for the stroke. All outstanding tennis players have learned to take the ball on the rise because of the tactical advantage it offers, while beginners and most women seem to feel more sure of themselves when taking the ball at its peak or on the descent. Because it is difficult to time the swing for a rising ball, it is strongly recommended that beginning players try to hit the ball either at its peak or, if its peak is higher than your waist, then waiting for the ball to descend to belt level. However, as soon as you feel that you can, learn to hit the ball on the rise so you may use the advantage of the pressure of time it will put on your opponents. Professional Ken Rosewall has said that he believes it is this ability to stroke the rising ball which more than anything else will separate the good player from the average. Take the ball as early on its ascent as you can, but only as early as you can control it.

Four standards of all good ground strokes

At this point it may be well to recall and recognize some of the features common to the ground strokes of all effective players. Regardless of their individual discriminatives, all excellent tennis players execute their ground strokes with certain universal techniques. The four most important factors of these techniques are as follows.

(1) *They all maintain about a 45 degree angle between the racket handle and their forearm throughout the swing, most notably at the time of contact with the ball.* This is true regardless of the height of the ball when they hit it. Even if the ball is low, they bend their knees to bring their hand down low, keeping the racket head relatively high, to maintain the racket-forearm relationship at about 45 degrees.

(2) *All skilled players meet the ball early, at the front surface of their body, rather than waiting for the ball to get behind them (and thus hitting late).* This is often referred to as hitting "off the front hip," and is a twofold product of having the weight moving forward (toward the net), so that at contact it is largely on the front foot, and of meeting the ball with a laid-back wrist.

(3) *At impact with the ball the racket head is accelerating rather than slowing down or maintaining a constant speed.* In sports terminology, this is called "hitting through the ball," and by laws of physics it determines that the racket will be in charge of the direction of the ball instead of the momentum of the ball overpowering the racket at impact.

(4) *This accelerating racket head results in a follow-through that is longer than the backswing.* The day of the big backswing is gone. Instead, the better players take a relatively short backswing, then

bring the racket into the ball with accelerating speed, and carry the racket "through the ball" into a long follow-through that comes to rest quite naturally, without any forceful stoppage of the motion. In most cases, when inexperienced players complain that the ball seems to be heavy and turns the racket in their hand at impact, they will tighten up on their grip in an attempt to overpower the ball. In reality the cause is almost always that they are not accelerating the racket into the ball.

One more factor merits attention, although it is less defined. The swings of all excellent tennis players are unhurried, mainly because they prepare the racket early by getting it into the backswing before the ball has come upon them. But then, time allowing, there is a finite pause in their motion, never an actual halt, during which they set their sights on the approaching ball, sizing up their target. There is no true arrest in their motion, no real delay in momentum, but more a collection of impetus, coordination, and timing for the excution of the foreswing. Its effect is similar to the baseball infielder who, having taken a ground ball, then briefly discerns the position of his baseman before releasing his throw. It is also like the hunter who sights his prey, raises his weapon, and takes a quick fraction of time to aim before he fires.

IMPARTING SPIN TO THE BALL.   Stroking the ball to apply spin is often considered an advanced skill, when in actuality the technique is relatively simple and so natural that beginners can easily learn it. Essentially, it involves bringing the racket into the ball either on an upswing or a downswing instead of hitting flat. A flat drive is one in which the racket is traveling, at impact, generally parallel to the court with its face perpendicular, and the struck ball will have no pre- dominant type of spin. If the ball is met on an upswing, that is, the racket approaching the ball from below and meeting it while traveling upward, the resulting drive will be a topspinning ball. If the ball is struck on the downswing, with the racket approaching the ball from above and meeting it while traveling downward, the ball will have backspin.

A backspinning ball will be more stable in its flight, less affected by air currents, and will slow up on its bounce. A topspinning ball will have a tendency to dip into the court after it crosses the net and, in contrast to the backspun ball, will "kick" toward the back of the court after its bounce. A flat drive will travel on essentially a straight path in flight and will not bounce as high as either of the other two.

To backspin a ball, simply take the racket into its backswing higher than normal, then come down on the ball, finishing the swing with the racket head below the point of contact. Tilt the racket face slightly back to assist the spin, keep your elbow low, and try to hit the lower portion of the ball. Imparting topspin involves just the opposite technique. Close the racket face slightly (tilt it forward), then bring the racket into the ball from below and finish off the stroke higher than normal. Start the swing with your knees flexed, then unbend your knees in the stroke, and drop the right shoulder just before the foreswing to assist the motion.

Most players, even beginners, have a natural tendency to undercut their backhands and swing up on their forehands. While all tennis players should learn to hit flat on both ground strokes, the natural inclination to spin the ball should also be utilized. For the backhand,

Producing spin on the ball.

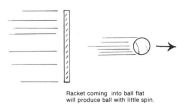

Racket coming into ball flat
will produce ball with little spin.

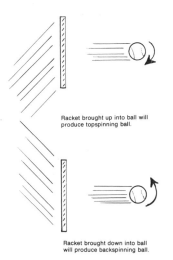

Racket brought up into ball will
produce topspinning ball.

Racket brought down into ball
will produce backspinning ball.

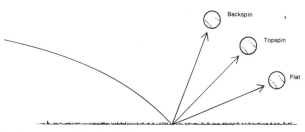

Backspin

Topspin

Flat

The bounce of the ball from the court.

This sequence of drawings illustrates the volley. (See text beginning on page 55.)

normally the least accurate of the two strokes, imparting backspin gives the advantage of stable ball flight. Topspinning the forehand drive allows one to hit the ball harder since it will dip downward in its flight, and in addition it will run off the court away from your opponent after the bounce. It must be understood, however, that the magnitude of spin you put on the ball, and consequently how hard you will cut your backhand and swing up on your forehand, depends entirely on what you can control.

(*Text continued on page 44.*)

Imparting topspin to the ball from the backhand, and backspinning a forehand drive both involve unnatural stroking motions. Besides, the grips are not conducive to hitting the ball in this manner. Both can be learned, however, but before any player attempts such spin, he must first learn to backspin the ball from the backhand and topspin the forehand.

The Serve

Early players of tennis considered the serve as nothing more than a method for getting the ball into play. It was an unglamorous part of the game that lacked the realization of its true offensive possibilities. But Maurice McLoughlin changed all that when he used a steady diet of blistering serves to win the 1912 U.S. Championship and set the tennis world to re-examining its ideas of the potential of the serve. No one had seen such power before, but nearly every tennis champion since McLoughlin has utilized the serve as a principal attacking weapon. It was said that Bob Falkenburg won the 1949 Wimbledon with the serve as his only ammunition, and ten years later Neale Frazer did much the same. In his prime Ellsworth Vines could average two to three aces a game, even in championship play! Jack Kramer owned a serve that would come across the net at 110 MPH, and Pancho Gonzáles could send the ball on its way at 113 MPH, perhaps the fastest ever.

This is not to imply that a strong serve excludes the necessity for developing the other strokes, but for better tennis it is the one essential skill among all others. Some professional tennis players have estimated that more than 50 per cent of the points in a match are scored as a direct or indirect result of the serve. Recent statistics compiled in championship matches have revealed that the serve does indeed win more points outright than any other stroke, and although it would not show in a count of points-won-by-various-strokes, the serve is often indirectly responsible for a point by forcing an opponent out of position or by inducing a weak return that can be volleyed away easily.

It's not unreasonable to expect to win at least 75 per cent of the games you serve. Each serve gives you complete control of the pace of the game, with your opponent totally dependent on your moves. Your serve must demand from him only the very best, and when it is working you will find it adds a surprising amount of confidence to the rest of your game.

Serving is throwing, and to serve well one must be able to throw well. In this respect girls have a genuine disadvantage. American boys have generally grown up with plenty of experience in throwing activities like baseball, football and even basketball. But in our culture throwing is rarely a natural attribute of women. Since many women players do not have the background of throwing to incorporate into the serve, this part of the game often is difficult for some to learn.

If you have never served (or never served well), learn the mechanics of the stroke by first taking a throwing stance (without the racket) behind the base line, and throw some balls into one of the opposing service courts. Notice that the higher you release the ball, the "lower" the net is since the angle into the service court is greater. Now take a ball in your left hand and push it into the air above your forehead, then "throw" your right hand up to the ball and catch it just as it begins to descend. Next, swat the ball with an open palm toward the net or to someone standing 15 to 20 feet in front of you. Finally, take the racket in your hand with a forehand grip, and use the racket face as an extension of your palm to hit the ball over the net.

Next, learn to toss the ball correctly for the serve. It is imperative that it be the same every time, otherwise the serve will be inconsistent. A faulty toss is responsible for as many serving errors as is any other factor. Until you can "sit" the ball in the air at the same place with every toss, your serving motion will be different every time.

Take a throwing stance again, then *hold the ball between the first two fingers and the thumb of your left hand (not down in your palm) and rest your ring finger alongside the ball.* Hold the ball (with your palm up) at about waist level and slightly in front of and to the inside of your left foot. With an underhand *lifting* (not a circular) motion, give the ball a boost straight up in the air, *releasing it when your arm reaches a comfortable extension.* Let the ball lift out of all your fingers at the same time (do not "flip" the ball), opening your hand as if you had "sticky fingers." Let the ball drop to the court, landing just in front of and slightly to the right of your left foot. As a target, lay your racket on the court with the face at the spot the ball should land, then practice the toss until you can consistently bounce the ball off the strings.

The height of the toss is just as important. To find your own correct height, extend your racket straight up as high as you can reach. Then toss the ball up to the racket so that if the tip were a ledge, you could settle the ball on that ledge. Lay the racket aside and practice reaching that height with each toss, boosting the ball with no spin so that it "hangs" in the air. *Recognize that the height of the toss is governed by how fast you move your arm, not by a "flip" of the fingers at release.*

Now for the actual hitting motion. As the toss was learned first without the racket, mimic the hitting motion first without the ball.

The backscratching position used in the serve.

Take a throwing stance again, with the racket in a forehand grip, and bring it over your right shoulder (with your wrist cocked) to a position that would allow you to scratch the small of your back with the head of the racket ("backscratching" position). *The butt of the racket points up, your wrist is almost behind your neck, and your elbow points off to the right and is raised so that your upper arm is level with the court.* Arch your back somewhat, rest your weight on your back foot, and face your shoulders parallel to the side line.

From this "backscratching" position the foreswing is based on sequential timing of body actions. *First, press your weight upward and forward, coming up on the toes of both feet. Then begin an upward and forward rotation of your right shoulder, and follow that in an instant by a lifting of your elbow. Fling the head of the racket upward and forward by unbending your elbow and wrist simultaneously. At the peak of the swing, your arm will be comfortably extended, but not locked. The foreswing, then, is both an upward and forward thrust that resembles the motion of pulling an arrow from a quiver.* From the peak of the swing, allow the racket to travel freely around in front of your body, arm remaining extended, and finish with the racket to the *outside* of your left leg.

At the height of the swing (the point at which you will meet the ball) your shoulders have pivoted around to face the net, your rear foot has come forward dragging the toe so that it is even with the left, and the strain of your weight is born entirely by the toes of your left foot. Then, as your racket continues on around, your weight "falls" into the court as a step is taken with the right foot to regain balance.

Some teachers of tennis suggest that there may be even a more preliminary stage for learning to serve. Take the racket in a western grip, bring it to the back of your shoulder (about parallel with the court), and simply swat the tossed ball as best you can. This technique does indeed appear to provide beginning servers with some success, but to develop any power at all on the served ball, the western grip will need to be abandoned at some time in the future.

When you have developed the rhythm of the foreswing, next learn how to get the racket into the "backscratching" position from the preparatory stance. It can be done in essentially two ways: either it can be taken up and over the shoulder (commonly known as the half-swing), or it can be taken down in a pendular motion and then around in back of your body.

THE HALF-SWING. Take the throwing stance again, weight even on both feet, and hold the racket in front of you much as you do for the ready position before the ground strokes, but for the serve you are standing erect. For the half-swing, all you need do is draw the racket up and over your right shoulder as you would a heavy hammer (the entire serving motion itself is often compared with the action of driving a nail). Arch your back as you draw the racket around to give yourself the feeling of a buildup of potential energy like the winding of a spring, with your weight on your back foot. This movement is the easiest way to get the racket into hitting position, and is a simplified version of the circular action most players use. However, many tennis teachers believe that this movement is all that a beginning or intermediate player needs to master in order to have an effective serve. Moreover, it appears that the half-swing serve is an especially efficient motion for women players, and therefore is to be strongly recommended for them.

Before we consider the full-swing serve, we need to add the toss to the half-swing. In the preparatory stance, cradle the throat of the racket in one or more fingers of your left hand, then *begin the action of both arms simultaneously; the left arm upward for the toss, and the right arm upward and backward to draw the racket into hitting position. Whip the racket up and forward to meet the ball just as it begins to descend.* What you are doing is simply putting together the two motions you have learned separately, but the coordination of the two will often give beginners a great deal of trouble. Unfortunately, there is no secret way to learn the total rhythm except to practice it repeatedly.

(*Text continued on page 52.*)

THE FULL SERVE. In the full windup serve, the racket travels down, alongside, and around in back of your body. Again, both arms start simultaneously, the left arm up for the toss, and the right arm down for the swing. This action is similar to swimming the side stroke. (Some players, however, will begin the swing an instant before the toss.) *The racket then continues on a pendular path, arm extended, to pass your right side and move around in back of you to shoulder level. At this point the elbow bends and the wrist cocks to bring the racket head to the backscratching position.* The total action is perpendicular, and in one big sweeping circle. One of the biggest problems with the swing is that of the weight transfer. Most beginners will bring their weight properly to the back foot as the swing starts, but many do not realize that *when the racket reaches the bottom of the swing the weight starts forward.*

It should be recognized that the full windup serving motion is rapidly losing popularity among top-flight players. In reality there is no mechanical advantage to the full windup, save that of possibly developing momentum. When studying the serving motion of better players, one discovers that there is no common mechanical technique to their bringing the racket into hitting position. Instead it is a study in contrasts. Most will draw the racket back at about waist level, but some still use the full windup and some even employ an exaggerated half-swing. It appears, then, that the windup is entirely a matter of personal choice, or, to each his own. However, every one of the players, without exception, will execute the following two actions. *No matter how they draw the racket back for the backswing, at some time in the swing they arrive at the classic "backscratching" position. And, once the windup is under way, there is never a distinct pause in the developing momentum of the swing.*

THE FLAT AND THE TOPSPIN SERVES. There are different fashions in which the ball can be stroked in the serve. They vary basically according to how the racket face is brought into the ball. Two of the methods should be learned by all tennis players: the flat and the topspin serves.

To topspin the serve, the racket face is closed and drawn up and over the ball, imparting a spin that dips the ball into the court as it crosses the net, then kicks forward off the bounce. The flat serve is hit with the racket face square to the ball, like swatting a fly, and the resulting ball flight is straight.

The eastern forehand grip is employed for the flat serve. As the name implies, the racket is brought into the ball "flat," with no effort to impart spin. Sometimes called the cannonball, it is used more than one might imagine in top play, but its demand for precise control makes it often a difficult serve for the average player to master. Short men and all women players seldom use the flat serve as their main weapon, but instead rely more often on the topspin.

There are two basic changes that need to be made for the topspin serve. *First, the ball is tossed slightly more to the right and back further (toward the right shoulder) than for the flat serve. Second, the grip used is the continental.* As your strength and timing improve on the topspin serve, your grip should begin to approach the eastern backhand (most top players use a grip between the backhand and the continental), but whatever grip you use the important thing is that *the thumb must not be allowed to run up the handle but must be laid diagonally across the handle instead.*

The difference in hitting the flat and topspin serves can be compared again to throwing a baseball. A flat serve is like throwing a fast ball; the hand is directly in back of the ball to utilize the full force of its power; in serving, the racket face is square in back of the ball. A topspin serve is like throwing a sinking curve ball: the hand is to the back and side of the ball at release and a snap of the wrist imparts the spin; in topspin serving, the continental grip and flick of the wrist will bring the racket to the back of the ball at contact, travelling upward and forward to impart the topspin.

The name of the serve again implies its hitting action, for the racket is brought into the ball like a knife to slice off the right upper portion, thus imparting a topspinning action on the ball. Such action requires a very flexible wrist. To get the feeling of this, take the racket with a continental grip, and dribble a ball on the court, each time brushing the strings along the right side of the ball by snapping your wrist downward. The sharply angled racket face will shoot the ball off to your left, but the spin will kick it right back to you again. This same wrist action is used for the serve. You must flick the racket head *up and over the ball to strike it a glancing blow. The racket head comes up to the ball and with its outside edge leading, tilted slightly toward the court, and moving slightly away from you, and at impact your arm still has not reached full extension.* To hit up and over the ball the racket at impact does not point skyward but is tilted at an angle to the left.

In reality, then, the racket actually strikes the ball while travelling an upward, forward, and slightly outward path. However, the kinesthetic feeling you receive when executing this action is that the racket is being brought up to and over the top of the ball to "yank" it down toward the service court. To re-emphasize, it is the brawny snapping of the wrist which adds the final explosive velocity to this action.

There should be one precaution. If the elbow leads the entire foreswing, so that at contact the elbow is pointing forward, the racket will be brought into the side of the ball instead of the back. Throughout the swing the elbow should point more or less to the sideline.

The violent wrist action will cause the racket head to lead the arm in the follow-through, and as for the flat serve, it finishes to your left.

The big advantage of the topspin serve is that it will break down toward the service court as it crosses the net, thus adding its own control factor. Men under six feet tall and all women must rely on it almost exclusively, but *all* players must learn to hit it.

THE AMERICAN TWIST SERVE. A third method of striking the serve is that known as the American twist. Sometimes called the kick serve, the spin is magnified, and the bounce is high and to the opponent's backhand. To execute the serve, the racket is taken with an eastern backhand grip, the ball is tossed slightly in back of the head, and then the racket comes up to meet the ball on its lower left surface. The wrist is snapped away from the body to impart the spin, and the follow-through is high and to the right of the server.

The American twist is used almost exclusively by the very best players as a second serve. However, it is extremely difficult for an average player to learn. The human arm simply was not made for the action it requires. Therefore, any efforts to learn the American twist serve should only come after the flat and topspin serves have been well mastered.

Practice of the serve

Despite the importance of the serve, it is seldom given its due in practice. A server must develop a rhythm that can be repeated time after time, as a skilled golfer can always duplicate his driving swing. Serving rhythm comes only with practice, and practice must be frequent.

Recognize first that there are two best places to stand. To insure maximum court coverage for the return of your serve, take a station near the center mark when serving to the deuce court (the right service court), and a few feet from the center mark when serving to the advantage court (the left service court). Always hit your practice serves from those two stations.

Get in the habit of keeping your left foot several inches behind the base line to avoid a foot fault. Remember that the rules forbid you to touch either the base line or the court before you hit the ball.

Practice the toss alone frequently, paying particular attention to its height. Too low a toss will cramp your serving motion, and too high a toss will cause you to hesitate waiting for it to descend. As Rod Laver has said, all players, even beginners, should learn to hit their serves when the ball is at the peak of the toss, or just after it has begun descending, for if you wait until the ball has dropped too far, it will be "heavy" on your racket. Experiment with his advice in practice.

If your serves are consistently too long, your toss may be back too far, or your wrist snap may be occurring too late. When the serves constantly finish in the net, the toss may be out too far, or your weight may be remaining on the back foot at contact.

When practicing the flat serve, make sure you get full extension of your arm at contact — very few players do. And girls especially need to concentrate on the follow-through, for there is a common tendency to pull up short in the swing and punch the ball. Remember that "falling" into the court is a natural after-effect of the serve and should be practiced since it will give you a sense of power.

If you find that you are not going up on the toes of your left foot when hitting, lift your heel off the court in your stance before you even start the swing, then keep it off throughout the backswing and foreswing. If your rhythm is poor, rocking back and forth several times before the swing seems to set up a proper cadence.

Finally, try especially for placements during practice instead of always crashing into the ball for speed. All techniques are worthless if the serve does not go in. A strong serve will make up for weak ground strokes, but if you have strong ground strokes and you cannot make your serves good, your ground stroke game will go unused.

The Volley

Tennis is far more than forehands, backhands and serves. Exclusive use of only the three-stroke game is basically a defensive strategy, and its potential for consistent success ends when you move up to playing rivals above the novice level. To own an aggressive offensive attack requires that you add the net game to your artillery, and the net game revolves around the volley.

The volley is an abbreviated ground stroke used to take a ball from flight before the bounce. It finds its greatest utilization from a position near the net as a follow-up to a strong serve or a well placed forehand or backhand. Often it is the decisive finishing stroke to a point. It so complements the serve that it can be said that an effective serve starts with placement and ends with the volley.

Aggressive singles play demands a mastery of the volley. Depending on your strategy you may find yourself using the stroke nearly as often as any other. In doubles the volley is even more important since the tactical objective of the game is to play from the net. Further, since beginning players often acquire their first tennis experiences via the doubles game, it is well for them to develop the volley quite soon in their learning.

The volley is to tennis what the bunt is to baseball. It's an exciting part of the game that is easier to learn than one might imagine. The motion is short and crisp, like a boxer's jab. To learn the volley take up a position near the net, feet comfortably spread and parallel.

Rest your weight slightly forward, keeping it off your heels, and crouch a bit. Lay the racket aside for now. Have someone stand across the net from you and toss some balls to your right and to your left, always within your reach. Catch all of them with your right hand. Then take your racket and repeat the practice, "catching" the ball with the strings instead of your hand. In this drill you are just trying to let the ball bounce off the strings and back to the tosser.

For the volley many good players use the continental grip, the advantage being that it requires no shifting of the hand from forehand to backhand, a sometimes difficult maneuver when the exchange of shots at the net is fast. If you use the continental grip for your ground strokes, keep that grip for the play at the net. However, most tennis players believe that if you use the eastern grip for the ground strokes you should first learn to volley with the eastern, and perhaps eventually slip into the continental. Using the eastern grip will require a quick adjustment from forehand to backhand, but as a beginner you can logically expect that the exchange of shots in your early competitive experience will not be so rapid that you do not have the time to switch. In any case, *the grip you use must be held tightly and with a rigid wrist.* In the backhand, you may want to run your thumb straight up the handle to use the extra bracing power it will give your grip. Otherwise, a strong shot may tear the racket from your grasp.

The ready position at the net is the same as it is for back court play, except that the racket head is held almost at eye level, and the weight is slightly forward. As in the ground strokes, *meet the ball with the racket head higher than the handle. Use no backswing, or reduce the backswing to a minimum by drawing the racket away from and then straight into the line of flight of the ball. Punch the ball forward and a bit downward by pushing the head of the racket flat into the ball.* You are trying merely to halt the progress of the ball rather than slam into it. In fact, the body position for a shoulder-high ball on the right resembles a policeman with his hand outstretched in a "halt" gesture.

Most outstanding players will under-cut the ball when they meet it. As a beginner, make no attempt to impart any spin to the ball, but as you gain in experience you will probably discover that a slight downswing in the volley stroke will become a very natural motion.

Take the ball in front of your body by reaching for it like a first baseman going after a throw. If the ball is several feet to one side, intercept its flight by using a cross-over step; that is, step across your body with the left foot to hit a ball on your right, and vice versa. The cross-over step not only extends your reach, it also rotates your shoulders to assist getting the racket into the proper hitting position. Often the speed of the ball does not allow you time to get into the classic volleying position, but if the volleyed ball goes inbounds, then all is well.

Correct body position for the volley. (See also the series of drawings beginning on page 62.)

Keep your body relaxed as you meet the ball, and always have your wrist inflexibly rigid at contact. Keep your eyes on the ball as it approaches, and meet it squarely in the center of the strings so its impetus does not turn the racket in your hand. As a practice drill to train your eye to the ball, try to actually get your head into a position for each volley so that you can look through the strings of your racket to see the approaching ball.

On balls which you are forced to meet below the level of the net, your volley must generally be a defensive stroke. All you can do is lift the ball over the net and hope for another chance. Tilt the racket face back to hit this volley, and punch the ball slightly upward. Bend your knees and lean over as much as necessary to keep the head of the racket higher than the handle.

On balls hit right at you, take them with a backhand. Push your elbow out to the right, loosen the grip slightly, and step back and away from the ball with your left foot to turn your shoulders. Do not expect to do any more than block these balls — the only ones you can kill are those that come to one side and above the level of the net.

Varying the direction of your backhand volley placements depends on what you do with your elbow. To dump a backhand to your left, push your elbow (not the racket head) out in front of you. To hit the ball to your right, keep your elbow in close. For the forehand, volleying the ball to the left requires meeting it early with the elbow back, and to hit to your right you must keep the head of the racket

back. If in a match you are ever in doubt as to where you should place
the volley, the safest place is up the middle of the court.

Be bold with the use of your volley, but not overanxious. If you
have developed some skill with the stroke, try to use a drive volley
(sometimes called a stroke volley). Its motion incorporates more of
a backswing and a bit of wrist action for a forceful punch at the ball
(but don't hammer away with all your strength). The drive volley can
be used only on a ball that comes to you above the level of the net.

Try never to volley on the dead run. Always set yourself before
you stroke the ball, and never attempt a finishing volley when you are
caught on your way to the net. Although the volley is an aggressive
stroke, you must be in an aggressive position to use it.

Like the serve, the volley seldom receives its justified practice
time. A fun way of doing your homework is to reduce the in-bounds
area to one service court on either side of the net, then play a game
in which you must hit the ball before it bounces. Another effective
learning game (using the full court) is to start a rally with both you
and your opponent at the base line, then both advance slowly toward
the net while trying to hit the ball directly at each other all the time.

HALF-VOLLEY. Sometimes you will be caught in a situation
where you must hit a ball just after it bounces. This calls for a half-
volley, a stroke made off a short bounce the way a baseball infielder
scoops a ground ball from a short hop or the way a football is drop-
kicked. It is a useful shot when you cannot get into position for any
other stroke. When hit from in front of the service line the half-volley
is always a defensive shot, but when hit from the back court it takes
on many of the qualities of a ground stroke, and can actually be used
as an attacking weapon. The execution of the stroke is relatively
simple and much more easy to learn than it appears to be.

When hitting a half-volley from a position close to the net, put the
strings behind the ball and *tilt the head of the racket back* to dump a
defensive shot across the net. Meet the ball just an instant after the
bounce, and with a stable wrist. *Get as close to the ball as you can by
bending your knees and leaning over toward the ball to keep from
making the stroke a "shoveling" motion.* Use no backswing at all, for
you cannot make a winner out of a half-volley from close to the net,
and be careful not to "lift" the ball with an upward swing; just let it
rebound from the strings.

From deep in your own court the half-volley is essentially a
ground stroke in which you need to drop the head of the racket down
in order to hit. The main ingredient for success is timing. Once you
have mastered it, the half-volley hit from behind your own service
line becomes an excellent stroke to use preceding a charge of the net.

DROP-VOLLEY. This shot is more difficult to master, and is used
only when your opponent is deep in his own back court and you are
in front of your own service line. To play the stroke, use a short back-

swing, and slide the strings of the racket across and down the back of the ball at contact. Relax the grip slightly, lay the face of the racket back a bit, and try to dump the ball just over the net.

Lob

There are two ways to pass an opponent who is stationed at the net: either to one side or over his head. Often men believe that women players should take the high road and they the low. There seems to be an impulse common to males to bash away at the ball regardless of the situation.

The lob is far from the sissy shot some stereotype it to be. All the professionals use it, as does any finished player. It can be used either as an outright winner or as a defensive measure, and thus there are two situations which call for its use. When your rival has camped at the net, a lob will free him from his site and perhaps win the point; these can be considered offensive lobs. When a well placed shot from your opponent's racket has driven you off the court, the lob will give you the necessary time to recover your position; these are defensive lobs.

The use of the lob can drag down a strong hitter and keep him from playing his type of game. As lobs come his way his nerves may begin to start working and he may press himself into overanxious errors.

Let the racket do the work for you in a lob. There is no need to lift your whole body into the shot—just hit both upward and forward. The grip is the same as for the ground strokes, for the lob is really a ground stroke hit into the air. *Compact the swing, shortening the backswing especially and restricting the shoulder turn, but get your racket under the ball and follow through in the direction you want the ball to go—high!* Tilting the racket face back helps, and a flick of the wrist completes the stroke.

Avoid attempting to put spin on the shot at first, but as time goes along you may want to try to hit your offensive lobs with topspin. Remember that the offensive lob is used to take a man from the net and put him behind the base line, so if the ball is topspun it will kick away from him off the bounce. *Keep offensive lobs low, just over the reach of your opponent's racket.* Hit them cross-court to the far corner, where there is more vacant court. Your objective is to stroke the ball so that it outruns your rival for a point winner, but even if he retrieves the ball you should by this time have taken up a position at the net yourself, for his return probably will not have his full power behind it. Moreover, it is likely that his return will itself be a lob. The best place to put lobs is over your opponent's left shoulder, making him hit a high backhand if he gets to the ball, the most difficult shot in tennis and one that should always invite your net charge. Disguise offensive lobs, coming into them as a ground stroke, then giving the ball its lift. They are especially effective when your foe comes too close to the net.

Just as the offensive lob is kept low, the defensive lob must be hit high. You will use it when you're in an awkward position to recover your own court, so you need time. To get that time, throw a lob *at least 30 feet into the air.* This is never an outright winner and is hit only out of necessity, but it enables you to stay in the rally and fight for the point. Slicing the ball (giving it backspin) stabilizes its flight and gives you better control of the shot, but slicing should be used only if it is within your capacities to do it consistently.

Sometimes the lob is the only thing you can do when your opponent has dumped a drop shot just over the net and you must charge in to retrieve it, arriving just in time to keep the ball from its second bounce. But other than that one circumstance, *no lobs should be hit from inside the fore court.* When you are that close to the net a passing shot will be more effective (if your opponent is also at the net), or, if your opponent is on the base line, hit a cross-court shot or a drop shot just over the net.

Learn the lob, especially if you are getting your first tennis experience by playing doubles, in which it is a basic weapon. Keep the balls deep but be careful not to overhit. Begin by hitting tossed balls low and short, gradually increasing the length and height of the ball. Later, have someone hit to you from a position at the net so you can lob over his head. Finally, have a rally with one player stationed at the net and the other at the base line. Learn especially the touch of just topping the reach of the net man, otherwise, your match opponents will smash away your too-low lobs.

When a ball is hit over your head and you are forced to hit a high backhand or forehand while on a dead run going away from the net, switch to the grip opposite to the one you would normally use (a forehand grip to hit the high backhand and vice versa), remember to get plenty of wrist snap, and throw your return shot extra high in the air.

Smash

Now for some real fun! If you are content to play a base line game you will probably see a lob come your way only once every third cycle of the moon, but if you enjoy the spirited kind of tennis that turns your blood a little redder you will frequently get yourself to the net. From this spot you will use the volley often, but will need to anticipate a lob from your opponent, and as a ready reply to the lob you must learn the smash. Any aggressive serve-volley player needs the smash in his bag of tricks, and if his serve is strong enough to enable him to use the net charge, then he can easily learn the smash because of its close resemblance to the serve.

The smash is a real sporting shot. It is hit for an attempted winner every time. There's an air of finality about the stroke and, when successful, it leaves the striker with a sense of assurance about the rest of his game, like the golfer who belts that long, straight drive and suddenly inherits new confidence from it. And it's not just a man's stroke, for women can do it too. Try it! Learn it! If you can hit a decent serve you can also smash.

The difference between the serve and the smash is that the ball just isn't where you want it for the smash, you have to go get it, and therein lies the first essential to the smash. *You must get under and in back of the ball, with your whole body under control, so that you can hit* down *on the ball.* Get into position, body side-on to the net but not pulled around as much as for the serve, for there is less body rotation in the smash than in the serve. Come to a ready position and keep both feet on the ground instead of leaping as the pros do. *Keeping your eyes intently on the ball, draw your racket back, weight to the rear foot, bend your back, and lift your non-hitting hand toward the ball as a sort of gun sight. Rise to your toes as you stroke the ball, coming through with a wrist snap that sends the racket head more forward than your wrist at contact to keep from hitting the ball out of bounds. Arm fairly straight at impact, your body jackknifes forward to increase power. Do not wind up as much as you do for the serve; always draw the racket back in a half-swing manner rather than a full-windup.*

Learn to smash first by punching at the ball, gradually increasing the length of your swing and the force of the stroke. The grip can be either the eastern forehand or the continental, but avoid slipping into the western grip unknowingly. Try for accuracy in placing the ball toward the corners, for the shot is not based on power alone. Develop the ability to hit this morale-building stroke from any place on the court, but remember that the further you are from the net, the less angle you have and therefore accuracy at the sacrifice of power is the call.

Begin first by hitting tossed balls into the fence. (Toss them up yourself instead of having someone do it for you.) Then move to the court for your trials, finally playing a lob-smash game with a partner who lobs to you while you answer with a smash. Remember as you practice that *you must flick the wrist to get the racket head facing downward at impact, but that the first racket movement in the foreswing is upward to extend the arm, as in the serve.*

Although in a match you may be hungry for an opportunity to display your ability to crash into the ball, be cautious of those very high lobs. When the ball comes descending to you from nearly a vertical drop it cannot be smashed without good timing. Let this one bounce first, then hit it, even though the wait gives your opponent the time he wanted to recover his position. Often these balls will bounce high

(Text continued on page 66.)

enough so that they can be smashed anyhow. Do not attempt a ground stroke off the bounce. And remember, if you do try to smash a sharply falling ball and you miss completely in your swipe at it, the rules do not call you out for this one strike. Recover and try again from the bounce.

Seldom will you ever need to hit a backhand smash, but when you must, meet the ball more out in front of your body, keeping accuracy in mind. Especially on the novice level, even a moderately hit smash is seldom returned. As for any stroke, the first requirement is that the shot go in: avoid hitting too hard and try for the corners or the feet of your opponent in a match. When you reach the point that you can consistently place the ball with accuracy, then take the advice of Charlie Hollis, Australia's well known tennis coach: Forget the details — hit the bloody thing! Do what the word says — smash it!

Dinks

Seemingly, anything that is left over after considering the major strokes falls under the category of dinks, that is, shots hit softly, away from your opponent, and often with a great deal of spin. The chop is such a shot. It is hit with a hatchet-like swing at the ball and with a loose grip. Generally, it is lifted just over the net when an opponent is deep, and the backspin on the ball will tend to bounce it toward the net, or away from your rival. Drop shots are also lofted just over the net, but they are hit without spin by simply laying the racket in back of the ball and allowing it to carom off the strings (again, with a loose grip). Both the drop and the chop can actually be used as attacking weapons and outright point winners, but they should be employed only when they are under your full control, otherwise they will be sitting ducks for your opponent. Never try them against a player who is at the net, and never try to hit them from the fly. Remember to always let the ball bounce first.

4

The Rules and
Scoring of Tennis

An official Code of Rules to standardize tennis play throughout the world was set down in 1912 by The International Lawn Tennis Federation, and has remained essentially unchanged since that time. Member countries of the ILTF are individually cast with the responsibility of interpreting and enforcing the rules in their own land. In this country the function of supervising play is carried out by The United States Lawn Tennis Association, an ILTF member. The rules which govern tennis in the United States are presented here in a non-technical manner along with some customs which have become complementary to those rules.

THE SINGLES GAME

THE PLAYERS AND THE RIGHT OF SERVICE. The player who delivers the ball at the start of a point is called the server, and the other the receiver. One player remains as the server for all points of the first game of a match, after which the receiver becomes the server for all points of the second game, and so on alternately for all subsequent games of the match.

The right to be the server or the receiver, or to have the choice of sides, is to be decided before the match "by toss." No stipulation is given in the rules as to how this toss is to be made. Tradition has established the spin of a racket as the usual method. For this spin, the players select some identifying mark which is on one side of the racket but not the other, or perhaps a trade mark on the end of the racket. One player then "spins" the racket while the other calls his choice, much like calling heads or tails in a coin flip.

The player who wins the toss is allowed to choose the side of the net he prefers, *or* he may choose whether to serve or receive. Note that winning the toss does not automatically mean that that player will serve, for he may instead declare his intent to receive in the first game. However, whenever the winner of the toss elects to be *either* the server or the receiver, then the choice of sides is given to the other player. If the winner of the toss declines his first option and instead chooses a side, then the right to be the server or the receiver is given to the other player.

DELIVERY OF THE SERVICE. The server must take up a position behind the base line without touching that line, and between an imaginary extension of the center mark and the *singles* side line. From that location he must project the ball into the air by hand and strike it in any fashion with his racket before it hits the ground. Although it would be impractical, the service may legally be made sidearm or underhand. The delivery is deemed to have been completed at the instant the racket contacts the ball.

ALTERNATING COURTS. For each point the server is given two opportunities to make one good service into the proper court. To start a game, the server stands to the right of the center mark and attempts to deliver the ball diagonally across the net into the receiver's right service court. When the first point has been completed the server then stands to the left of the center mark and attempts to deliver the ball into the receiver's left service court, and so on alternately until all points of the game have been completed. Thus, when the total number of *completed* points is an even number (none, two, four, etc.), service attempts are made from the right of the center mark, and when the total number of *completed* points is an odd number (one, three, five, etc.), service attempts are made from the left of the center mark.

If a player inadvertently serves from the wrong side of the center mark, all play resulting from that wrong service or services is to be counted, but the improper position of the server must be corrected as soon as it is discovered.

FAULTS. A fault is an invalid serve, and is alway counted as a service attempt. The *foot fault,* the most common violation of all the service rules, occurs when the server steps on the base line or into the court before his racket contacts the ball, or when the delivery is made from a station that is not between an extension of the center mark and the singles side line. The server may legally have any part of him *over* the base line or the court during the delivery, but may not *touch* the base line or the court until the completion of the delivery (when the racket meets the ball). A foot fault can also be called when the server changes his original position by walking or running during the delivery, although this is a very rare occurrence. A recent rule change no longer requires that the server have one foot in contact with the ground at the moment the racket meets the ball. Thus, the serve may legally be made while the server is completely in the air, not in contact with the ground at all.

Another service fault occurs when the server swings the racket with the intent of striking the ball but misses. However, the server may toss the ball into the air and then catch it or allow it to fall to the court without penalty, so long as he does not attempt a delivery of that ball. A poorly tossed ball does not need to be served, but instead can be tossed again.

Finally, the service is a fault if the delivered ball does not land in the proper service court or on a line bounding that court, or if the ball touches a permanent fixture (other than the net) before it hits the court. If a served ball touches the net on the way to the proper service court it is not a fault but is considered instead to be a let.

THE LET. When a legally delivered service hits the top of the net and then lands in the proper service court or on a bounding line of that court, the service is a let and *that service only* is retaken. In addition, a let may be called by the receiver if he was not ready to receive the serve. The server must, prior to each delivery, always allow time for the receiver to assume a position of readiness. However, if the receiver makes an attempted return of the serve it is considered that he was ready.

Any other interruption in normal play from an outside source is also a let, and the point is replayed. For example, if a ball from a neighboring court interrupts a rally or either of the services, the *entire point* is replayed including the two service opportunities for the server, even if the interruption occurred during the second service.

RECEIVING THE SERVE. There are no rules that govern the position of the receiver; he may stand wherever he chooses, including within the service court. However, he may not strike the served ball for an attempted return until after it has bounced, and he must strike the ball before it bounces twice, otherwise a point is automatically awarded to the server.

CONTINUOUS PLAY. Unless a fault or a let is called, a ball which is delivered in service is in play at that moment and remains in play until the point is decided. Play is continuous as long as the players succeed in returning the ball either from the service or during play following the service, and even though a return may strike another ball lying within the boundaries of the court. As is true with the service, a ball which lands on a line is considered to have landed in the court bounded by that line. After the service, it is not necessary for the player to let the ball bounce before he makes an attempted return. He may instead strike (volley) the ball from flight.

GOOD RETURNS. A player has made a good return and play continues:

1. When the ball lands from flight within the proper court.
2. If the ball strikes and passes over the net, post or any part thereof, and then lands within the proper court.

3. If the return passes outside the post, either above or below the level of the net, and then lands within the proper court, even if it touches the post during its flight.

4. When the player's racket passes over but does not touch the net after making a good return, provided that the player struck the ball from his own side of the net.

It should be pointed out that, regarding number 4, a player is obliged to allow the ball to pass to his side of the net before he may make an attempted return. However, *if the ball has bounced in his court,* and the spin of the ball causes it to rebound or it is blown back over the net again, the player may legally reach over the net to strike the ball provided that neither he, his clothes or racket touch the net or the opposing court.

AWARDING OF POINTS. The server wins a point when his legal service is not returned, or when his service hits the receiver or his racket before it touches the ground. The receiver wins a point when the server commits two consecutive faults (a double fault) or otherwise delivers the ball in an illegal manner.

After the service, a player loses a point:

1. When the ball bounces twice in his court before he strikes it.

2. When his return lands outside the opposing court or hits a permanent fixture (other than the net, post or any part thereof) before it touches the ground. However, it must be recognized that if a return hits a permanent fixture (other than the net, post or any part thereof) *after* it has bounced, the point is automatically given to the player who made the return.

3. Any time he strikes a ball before it has bounced and fails to make a good return, even though he was standing outside the boundaries of his own court when the ball was struck.

4. If he hits the ball more than once for each attempted return.

5. If he, his clothing or his racket touches the net, the post or any part thereof while the ball is in play.

6. If he volleys a ball from flight before it has passed to his side of the net.

7. If the ball in play touches him or anything that he wears or carries except his racket. A return may legally be made off any part of the racket.

8. If he throws his racket at and hits the ball.

9. If he intentionally interferes with his opponent making a stroke.

SCORING. The system of scoring in tennis differs from all other sports. A player must first win at least four *points* to win a game, then at least six *games* to win a set, and usually at least two *sets* to win a match. In scoring for each game the points are not counted in their numerical order of 1, 2, 3 and so on. Instead, when a player has no points his score is called *love*; when he wins his first point his score is called *15* (some players erroneously refer to the first point as 5); on winning his second point his score is called *30*; on winning his third point his score is called *40*; and on winning his fourth point he has won the *game,* provided that he is ahead by at least two points at that time.

When both players have won one point the score is called *15 all, and when both players have won two points the score is called 30 all,* but when both players have won three points the score is called *deuce.* A score of deuce means that one player must win the next two consecutive points to win the game. The first point won by a player after a deuce score is called *advantage* for that player (often shortened to *ad).* If that point was won by the server it is called *ad in,* and if that point was won by the receiver it is called *ad out.* If the same player who won the advantage point also wins the next point, the game is won by that player. However, if the other player wins the next point, the score returns to deuce, and so on until one player wins two consecutive points after a deuce score.

This unusual system of counting points has been traced to eighteenth-century France when, for the benefit of spectators, players' scores were recorded on a large clock face kept at courtside. As each point was decided, a hand was moved one-quarter of the clock face, and the game was won when the hand came back to the starting point. Thus, points came to be known as 15, 30, 45, and game. No one knows why the 45 evolved to be called 40 in the contemporary scoring.

The French were also responsible for the terms "love" and "deuce." Love is derived from the French word, l'oeuf, meaning the egg, or zero. Deux is French for two, or an advantage of two points.

Perhaps the scoring system will be more easily understood without its terminology. Quite simply, if a player wins four points before his opponent has won three, he wins the game. If the score becomes tied at three points each, then the game is not won until a player has a two-point advantage.

There is even a more basic scoring technique: the VASSS, or Van Alen Simplified Scoring System, named after its originator, Jimmy Van Alen. It has not received any wide-spread acceptance at all. There are several varieties of the system, but in the most practical of them, points are counted as 1, 2, 3, and 4. As in traditional scoring, a player winning 4 points with at least a 2-point advantage wins the game, and with a score tied at 3-all one player must win the next two points to finish the game. The big difference is that if the score becomes tied at 4-all, the player who wins the next point wins the game. In effect, then, there is no deuce or ad in any game.

When a player wins six games and has at that time a lead of at least two games, he wins the set. If a player wins six games and his opponent has won at least five games, the set is extended until one player has a two game lead.

The Tie-breaker. A controversial change from the traditional set-settling rule requiring a two-game advantage is the tie-breaker, also an invention of Van Alen's. The tie-breaker eliminates prolonged sets, and can wrap up a match when the clock signals the end of a time period on a busy court. It consists of winning 5 of 9 points (strongly recommended by the USLTA), or winning 7 of 12 points. Either can be used when a set becomes tied at 6 games all. Each point of the tie-breaker has a numerical value of one. So, when a player wins the first point the score is 1–0. If he wins the next point the score is 2–0, and so on.

In the more accepted version, winning 5 of 9 points, if it is player A's turn to serve the 13th game (with the score tied at 6 games each), he serves points 1 and 2, right court and left court. Then player B serves points 3 and 4 (R and L courts). Players then change sides, and A serves points 5 and 6; B serves 7 and 8, until one player scores 5 points with a two-point advantage. If the score reaches 4 points all, player B serves point 9 *from the right or left court at the election of the receiver.* The set then becomes recorded as 7 games to 6. Player B becomes the server for the first game of the next set, and the players stay on their sides of the court for one game following the playing of the tie-breaker.

In the tie-breaker decided by 7 of 12 points, player A serves points 1 and 2 (R and L courts), player B serves points 3 and 4, and A serves points 5 and 6. Players then change sides. B serves points 7 and 8, A serves points 9 and 10, and B serves points 11 and 12. When either player reaches 7 points with a two-point advantage he has won the game. If the score reaches 6-all, the players change sides again and play continues with the serve alternating after every point until one player establishes a two-point margin, as follows: A serves the 13th point from the right court; B serves point 14 from the right court. If the game is not completed, A serves point 15 from the left court, B serves point 16 from the left court, and so on until a two-point advantage is attained. If the score remains tied, players change sides after every 6 points and continue. At the conclusion of the 7 of 12 tie-breaker play B is the server for the first game of the next set, and the players stay on their sides for that game.

The number of sets needed to win the match is usually determined beforehand by the players, or by tournament regulations. The official USLTA rules state that the maximum number of sets needed to win a match shall be three for men and two for women, although individual tournaments can establish their own criteria. Most informal matches are decided on the basis of the best two out of three sets.

CHANGING SIDES. Sometimes a tennis match is played where it is an advantage to be on one side of the net because of the sun, wind, hitting background, or some other reason. In order to equalize the advantages and disadvantages of the two sides, the rules require that the players change sides of the court at the end of the first, third, and every subsequent odd game of the match. If the *total* games played in the first set are an even number, the players remain on the same side of the court for the first game of the second set, and if the total games played in the first set are an odd number, the players change sides to start the second set. To determine the players' sides for the start of a third set, the total number of games played through the first two sets is counted, and so on for any subsequent sets.

The normal rotation of sides for subsequent sets becomes altered if a tie-breaker was played to conclude a previous set. Therefore, it is well to review and recognize the influence of this tie-breaker in determining sides for following sets.

THE DOUBLES GAME

The playing court for the doubles game includes the alleys, making it 4½ feet wider on each side than the court for the singles game. To deliver the ball in the service, the server may stand between an extension of the center mark and the *doubles* side line, an area that includes the extended alley. However, the service courts remain the same as those used for the singles game. All other rules for singles apply also to the doubles game with the following exceptions.

ORDER OF SERVICE. Both teams determine their order of service at the beginning of *each set,* and that order must remain the same throughout the set. One player of one team serves for the first game, and then that team becomes the receivers for the second game. The partner of the player who served in the first game then serves for the third game, and the partner of the player who served in the second game then serves for the fourth game, and so on for all subsequent games of the set, each player serving every fourth game. With the completion of the first or any subsequent set, a team may elect to change its order of service for the next set.

Should a partner serve out of turn, a correction must be made as soon as the mistake is discovered, but all play (including service faults) which has been completed before the discovery must be reckoned. If a game has been completed before the erroneous serving order is discovered, the order as altered must then remain for the continuation of the set.

ORDER OF RECEIVING. The order of receiving the service is decided by each team at the beginning of each set, and must remain the same throughout the set. The player who first receives in the right service court must continue to receive in that court for the entire set, and his partner must receive all serves in the left service court for the entire set. At the end of any set a team may change its order of receiving for the next set. The order of receiving in any set is *not* determined by the order of serving for that set; that is, the partner who served first is not required to receive first.

Should a team receive out of turn, the altered receiving order must remain as is until the end of the game in which the discovery is made, whereafter the partners must resume their original receiving order for the next game of that set in which they receive.

SERVED BALL STRIKING A PLAYER.   There are no restrictions as to where the partner of the server and the receivers must stand. Each may take up a position of his choice, but it must be recognized that if a served ball strikes the server's partner or anything that he wears or carries it is a fault, and if a served ball (which is not a let) strikes the partner of the receiver or anything which he wears or carries before it touches the ground, it is a point for the serving team.

PLAY AFTER THE SERVICE.   Each time the ball crosses the net any partner but one partner only may strike the ball for an attempted return. If both partners touch the ball with their rackets for any one return a point is awarded to their opponents.

The Tie-breaker.   Assume that players A and B are competing against players C and D, and that the set becomes tied at 6 games each. In a 5-of-9-points tie-breaker, the same sequence of events is followed as in singles. Player A serves points 1 and 2, player C serves points 3 and 4, and then the teams change sides. Player B then serves points 5 and 6, and player D serves points 7 and 8, until one team has won 5 points with a two-point advantage. If after 8 points the score remains tied, player D serves the 9th and deciding point. In a 7-of-12-points tie-breaker, player A serves points 1 and 2. Then the teams change sides, and continue to change every 4 points thereafter. Otherwise, it is the same as in singles. In both the 5-of-9 and the 7-of-12 the teams stay on their sides of the court for the first game of the next set after the tie-breaker.

CUSTOM AND COURTESY

As in any sport, the official rules of tennis govern only the technicalities of the game itself, while years of playing establish the unwritten customs and traditions. Tennis is always played in an atmosphere of genuine sportsmanship. In part, this is due to the very nature of the game itself, for the great majority of matches are played without the aid of linesmen, and each player is therefore cast with the responsibility of officiating his own side of the court.

Most of the behavior that is expected from players of tennis is a matter of common sense. Make your attire acceptable for the courts; a word to the men — keep your shirt on. Next, consider your neighbors on the next court. Avoid walking behind them when they have a ball in play. This is a most intolerable annoyance for those who are playing a point. If you must cross in back of an occupied court to get to the one you will be using, or if you need to retrieve a ball near their court, wait until the point they are playing has been completed. And, if during one of your rallies a ball strays into their court or one of theirs rolls to your court, again wait until the point is over before you ask for your ball or return theirs.

Even before the warm-up prior to the start of the match players customarily check the height of the net by placing one racket vertically next to the center strap and another horizontally on top (see sketch below). The net should equal the height of the two rackets.

During the formal warm-up before a match, it is wise to feed your opponent a variety of shots to discover how he handles them and thus to give yourself some cues for the planning of your strategy. However, this is not to be overdone. A few of each variety suffices, and the rest of the time your shots should be hit right to him with only moderate speed so that both of you may warm up properly. Should he request that you give him a certain type of shot it will be proper for you to oblige, and if there is a certain stroke that you want to practice it is permissible for you to ask for the kind of shots you need in order to practice that stroke.

Include the serve in your warm-up. Somewhere along the line many people pick up the erroneous idea that practice serves are to be taken by each player just prior to the first game he serves in. When you have the service, always start with two balls so that you will not need to chase after another ball to hit if you fault on your first attempt. Wait until your receiver is ready, particularly for the second serve, and offer to serve over again if it appears he was not. Try to avoid foot faults, even though no one is going to call them on you. As a server, it is your responsibility to announce the score after each point, always stating your own total first.

When receiving the serve, do not distract the server or stall unnecessarily. If a serve does not land in the proper court, call "fault" and do not return the ball. Making a habit of returning serves that are out is one of the most discourteous acts in tennis. Say nothing on the good serves; just play the ball.

Make the calls on your side of the net fairly, giving your opponent the benefit of the doubt on close ones. Do not contest his calls, even though he may seem a bit myopic (get another opponent next time instead). Play the point over when you are in doubt about a ball's being in or out. Sometimes you will have a better view of a ball that lands near a line on your opponent's court than he will (it happens often on serves), in which case he may ask you if it was in or out and the call is then yours to make.

Give your opponent his due credit for good shots instead of blaming yourself for allowing him to have them, and talk to him during exchanges of sides. Finally, regardless of how competitive your nature is, remember that this is a game, and take it as such.

5

Game Strategy

In the final analysis, the learning or improvement of tennis skills is ultimately and principally for the purpose of employing them in match play. There is a great deal of difference between the rehearsal of individual stroking skills and the proving ground of actual competition. Practice can only simulate a game. The real test of a player's ability to effectively combine and utilize his skills comes only through their direct application in the game itself.

Enter now the importance of the intellect. The courts are full of players who can hit a great game during practice but who fail to put their brain in gear when the match begins. By its very nature tennis demands that its participants be able to coordinate their physical and mental skills. All good competitors begin every match with a pre-planned strategy, then change it when necessary during play, and re-examine its rationality when the match is over.

Of course it is impossible to set down a single tactical formula for success that can be plugged in for all players. Even if one could, the fun of competition would be gone since each player would always know what his opponent was up to. Because everyone has developed different strengths, every player must adopt a game plan that suits his own personal bag of tricks. However, there are general principles of strategy that most players logically apply in given situations. Those stratagems revolve around four different aspects of the game: the service, the return of the service, net play, and base line play. And within each of these "smaller games" there are situations that are constantly repeating themselves throughout any match. Methods for handling those situations have been devised that have proved generally successful for the majority of players. These four aspects of the game in both singles and doubles follow.

THE SINGLES GAME

THE SERVICE. All too often inexperienced tennis players assume they should bash away at their first service attempt and, having failed, pat the second. Most novice players would do well to slow down their first serves and be more aggressive with their second offerings. *First serves need to be successful about three-fourths of the time, mainly to keep your opponent hitting from on or behind his base line, where his distance from your court is such that he is less likely to return a shot beyond your reach.* In addition a first serve which can be made consistently good is always a psychological boost to any server. Get into the right frame of mind for the first serve, hitting it every time with the confidence that it will win the point. Remember the most advantageous positions to serve from; near the center mark when serving into the deuce court, and a few feet from the center mark for the advantage court. *Have all your decisions about the service made before you begin the delivery—very few beginners ever do. Note the position of your receiver, then fix firmly in your mind the type of serve you will hit and the exact area of the court into which you will place it.*

Generally, *placements for the first serve are made deep to the far corner in both service courts, a strategy that pulls the receiver off the court to open up a wide area for a volley of his return.* Such far corner placements of the serve are most effective when followed with a rush to the net for a better volleying position, but this should be done only if the charge toward the net does not interfere with your ability to make the serve good, and only if you have control of your volley. Otherwise, it may be best to remain near the base line and take the ball from the bounce. A serve hit to the far corner of the deuce court will open up your opponent's weaker backhand side for a follow-up placement of his return, and when hit to the far corner in the advantage court the serve itself attacks the receiver's backhand, often winning the point outright or eliciting a soft return. A topspin serve is particularly effective in the deuce court (when placed in the far corner) since it moves away from the receiver both in flight and from the bounce. If you can hit an especially vicious spin you might try an occasionally shallow placement with it, but always along the side line.

Down-the-middle placements of the serve (parallel to the center service line) have the advantage of reducing the receiver's opportunity to return a cross-court shot. *Because it gets there very quickly, a flat serve is very effective for placements in the near corners, but keep in mind that a flat serve should never be hit unless it is hit with spirit, and this demands precise control.* Women and smaller men may want to attempt a flat serve only occasionally, and because it gets to the receiver faster than the topsin, a flat serve is almost never followed with a net rush. If you use the flat serve, keep mental notes of your opponent's response to it. Some receivers are happy to see a flat serve come their way, while others may be more bothered by it than the topspin serve.

A third area of placement for the first serve is right at the receiver. If you can hit the ball with a bit of ginger on it, the receiver may waste a fatal moment deciding whether to take the ball with his forehand or his backhand. A topspin serve that moves into a receiver will especially generate this indecision.

If your first serve is not particularly powerful and you notice that the receiver always manages to get his racket on the ball, you may subconsciously begin to press for more speed. But *if your serve is being only weakly returned, even though it is always being hit, forget about the ace and instead continue to serve just as you have been.*

The second service has four basic principles which govern its delivery. First, since there is nothing more destructive to a tennis player than habitual give-away points from double faults, the serve must always be good. Second, since the flat serve is so much more difficult to control, it must be a topspin; use the flat serve only very rarely for its potential surprise element. Third, since the second serve is hit at a slower pace than the first serve, it must generally be placed to the opponent's weaker side, usually the backhand (although not so constantly that the receiver can set himself for it). And fourth, to keep the receiver from moving in for an easy return that will give him both the offensive and the net, the second serve must always be kept deep. In his comprehensive text of *The Game of Singles in Tennis,* former U.S. Davis Cup Team Captain Bill Talbert cites statistics to prove that when the second service is kept deep (meaning within 3 feet of the service line) it wins the point about 75 per cent of the time, but when it is hit shallow the server can expect to win the point only about 50 per cent of the time.

The second serve must be under your control to the point that you have confidence that you could make it good every time, and if you have such confidence it will give you more freedom to try for a winner on the first serve. However, *if your second serve is continually being put away by your opponent, you will need to slow the first serve to get it in more often.*

Vary the pace and the placements of both services occasionally, for if you do not your opponent will prime himself for the kind of serve he knows he will receive. Try especially to get your first serves in at the start of a match; failure to make them good at that time may establish a faulty pattern. Also make sure you have warmed up properly before the match, hitting plenty of hard practice serves. Do not be discouraged by an occasional double fault, for they are often a sign of aggressive serving. Remember that the pace of the game is in your hands when you are serving; if things are going well for you keep a lively pace between the services, especially if there is a building frustration on your opponent's part; if things are not going so well take more time between the services (without actually stalling). Always *walk* back to your serving position for the next service. And finally, if you are starting a game just after you have won a game your opponent served (broken his serve), avoid the psychological letdown common to many players in this situation—even in advanced competition a player who breaks service often regards his accomplishment as an end in itself, then eases off on his game a bit and in turn has his own service broken.

THE RETURN OF THE SERVICE. There is no more neglected phase of tennis than the service return. Rarely is it ever practiced in itself, and when one considers the fact that every point in a match confronts one of the two players with the predicament of returning a service, it is even more difficult to understand why so crucial a situation can be so universally ignored.

The ready position for receiving the serve is the stance of an athlete: head up, a forward inclination of your back, flexion in your hips and knees, and weight off your heels. Spread your feet wide, a bit more than shoulder width. Point the racket at your opponent, elbows held comfortably in front of your hips. Cradle the throat of the racket in your free hand and hold its head at the height of your shoulders (to eliminate the wasted motion of raising it to that position in the backswing, and to reduce the feel of the weight of the racket in your hands). Finally, stand so that you face your opponent rather than keeping your feet parallel to the base line.

Most players wait for the service with the racket held in a forehand grip, but what you use is dependent on how easily you can change from one grip to the other. If, for example, you can switch from the forehand to the backhand grip more readily than vice versa (as most players can), then wait with the forehand. In any case, ease the tension in your hand as you wait. Some receivers will even spin the racket in their hands to keep from holding it too tightly.

Where you station yourself in preparation for receiving the serve will vary according to the talents of both you and the server. *There is no one best position for every situation, but keep in mind that your station must give you equal freedom to move either wide for serves hit in the far corners or toward the center mark for serves hit up the middle.* If your backhand is relatively weak you may want to crowd it somewhat, leaving more room on your forehand side. This usually places you two feet or so from the side line when receiving in the deuce court, and near the side line for receiving in the advantage court. If the server takes up his position further away from the center mark than is usual, you will need to change your station accordingly.

How far in (toward the service line) you stand to receive is influenced first of all by the speed of your opponent's serves. Girls seldom deliver the ball with enough force to push their opponents to a receiving position behind the base line, and even when a man's serve is rather patsy you will want to move well inside the base line to receive. But if your opponent can hit a real cannonball you must move deeper, sometimes even several yards behind the base line where the ball is not upon you so quickly, giving you more time to set yourself for the return. While this deep station invites a net charge from the server, very few players below the tournament level will continually follow their serves to the net, and even those who frequently do take the net will seldom do it behind a cannonball serve.

If you have developed the skill of taking the ball on the rise, your receiving station should always be rather shallow for three reasons: (1) any spin which the server imparts to the ball will have less time to work its effect; (2) since you will take the ball earlier you cannot be drawn as far off the court by a wide serve; and (3) there is less time for the server to charge the net, and even if he does you are in good position to hit a passing shot or to return the ball at his feet forcing him to volley up (hit the ball from below the level of the net). Talbert firmly believes that even beginners should learn to take the ball on the rise for the advantages it affords when receiving the serve. You will find the trick a bit easier to do on the slower second serve, your position for which is always several feet more shallow than it was for the first serve.

The speed of your opponent's serve will also influence the mechanics of your stroking action for the return shot. If the serve is not a particularly hard one you can swing the racket in much the same fashion you would use for any ground stroke, but *if your rival has a big serve you will need to abbreviate your swing, especially when taking the ball on the rise.* Use your left hand to push the racket into the forehand backswing or to pull it into the backhand hitting position, *bringing the racket only a little behind your shoulder.* The speed of the oncoming ball may not give you time to adjust your feet to a hitting stance, but there is always enough time to pivot your shoulders and hips so that you can stroke the ball rather than just block it. Come into the ball with a *very firm wrist* to capitalize on the power your opponent has already supplied for your stroke; a weak wrist will only dissipate that power. *The whole key to the stroke is how quickly you can get the racket into hitting position—thus the importance of the work done by the left hand.* The racket must have completed the backswing before the ball takes its bounce, and further, if you can draw the racket into the hitting position quickly, it may afford you a precious moment to pause at the end of the backswing and set your sights more firmly on the approaching ball.

Most service returns should be hit deep to the server's forehand or backhand corners. *Hard serves which come wide to your forehand in the deuce court and wide to your backhand in the advantage court are more easily returned with a down-the-line placement (a shot hit*

*parallel to the side line) for two reasons: (1) the ball can be taken later
— alongside your body rather than in front — giving you more time to
hit a complete stroke instead of just blocking the ball (a cross-court
attempt requires that the ball be met early — out in front of your
body), and (2) the down-the-line return does not so readily expose
one whole side of your court, which would give the server a wide
area for his follow-up shot.* Slower and more shallow serves (usually
second serves) are more inviting for cross-court returns since they
allow you the time to take the ball early and generally give a better
angle for shot placement. Keep in mind, however, that any service
return hit deep to the server's backhand will often force him to come
back with a softly hit shot which you can stroke either for an outright
winner or for a placement that will allow you to take the net. Drop
shots (balls just eased over the net so that they land near the net)
should be used only infrequently, and then only if you have excep-
tional control of them.

When you meet one of those rare players who follows his serves
to the net, deep placements to either corner are still effective returns.
However, his very act of charging the net now gives you a third area
to place the ball; right at his feet. Use the shot often, for *service returns hit low and right at the feet of a net rusher will force him to
volley up, usually resulting in a "floater" that you can often hit for
a point winning placement.* This strategy always reduces the server's
cross-court volleying opportunities, and if you can consistently return
his serves to his feet it may eventually discourage him from charging
the net in the first place.

Even more effective against the net-rusher may be a return hit to
either side of him that lands near the service line. Such a return not
only forces the server to volley up, but also makes him extend his
reach to do so. If the server has continued his forward charge and has
not "pulled up" as you are about to hit, a placement of the return to the
side of him, landing near the service line, may actually pass him by
and win the point.

Treat each serve as an individual event, giving the full attention
of your eye and mind to the ball as it comes off your opponent's racket.
Above all else, your prime objective is to get the return in-bounds.
If this means that you must resort to blocking the ball or hitting half-
lobs or any other defensive measure, then resort to them. It is especially important to make the returns good when you have a command-
ing lead in the score, for even if they are only softly hit shots your
opponent is less likely to try an aggressive placement on them when
he is far behind.

FORE COURT PLAY.   Inexperienced tennis players seldom spend
much of their game time at the net. Often this is because they believe
they do not own the necessary stroke repertoire for play in the fore

court, but just as frequently it is because they have not yet learned to respond to the opportunities for a net rush that are inherent in any match. While a strong net game is not so compulsory a part of the arsenal of a singles player as it is for a doubles team, its winning potential is often overlooked. All players, including the ladies, beginners, and youngsters, should learn to attack the net when they are given the chance.

Any trip to the net cannot be made haphazardly. *It is to be done only when an opportunity is presented, and must always be preceded by a forcing shot that will put your opponent on the defensive.* Excluding the serve, the first such opportunity for a net rush usually comes on a short ball. Generally, when you stroke a shot from near your own base line, you should remain in that vicinity following your shot, but when your rival invites a net charge by offering up a short ball (and the higher the bounce the better), then acknowledge the invitation. As you move in to retrieve the shallow shot, continue right on to a station at the net following your return. A word of caution here; *when hitting from a run, follow your shot to the net only if a continuation of that run will bring you into a volleying position.* When you are forced to retrieve a ball that leaves you moving away from the net, return to the back court and wait for another chance.

You must prepare your advance to the net by hitting a forcing shot that will cause your opponent to reply weakly. Generally, this calls for a deep placement to one of the corners, usually the backhand. Then, as you move to the net, drift toward the side of your placement to bisect the angle of the return; the wider your shot, the more you must crowd the side line. *A forcing shot hit deep to either corner usually results in a down-the-line return. Thus, you must anticipate that return in your volleying position.* When you have forced your opponent to hit from a position that is off the side of his court beyond the doubles side line, and he attempts to return cross-court, the ball will almost never cross the net on the opposite side of the center strap, and always such an attempt will leave him little room for error.

Going to the net following an approach shot must be done as quickly as possible, keeping your racket in readiness on the way. Study your rival as you move into the fore court, and *just as he is about to make his return shot, bring yourself to a controlled pause, ready to move in any direction for the ball.* At this time you may not yet be in the proper volleying position, and the shot that comes your way may force you to hit a defensive volley or half-volley. If so, put that volley deep down the middle to cut the chance of a cross-court shot, then finish off your move to the net.

Overanxious players are often so close to the net in anticipation of their opponent's return that they leave themselves vulnerable to the lob. The proper volleying position is *at least an arm-and-racket's length from the net.* From there you can easily step into a low return to volley down on the ball, and when your foe answers with a lob you are already in a better position to retreat. *Finish off the point as soon as possible, for that is what you came to the net to do. Be bold with your volley. Fling it out of reach of your opponent or, when you have him on the run, occasionally fire the ball into the area of the court he just vacated. Generally, volley a high ball deep and lift a low one just over the net. If ever you are in doubt about where to hit your volley always resort to a deep down-the-middle placement. And when your opponent feeds you one of those sitting lobs that ask to be smashed, let fly at the ball with some authority. Shell it either at the feet of your adversary or out of his reach, but hit it only as hard as you can control.* Keep in mind that overanxiety on these floaters often leads to netting the ball, and the further away from the net you are when you hit the smash, the more you must sacrifice power for accuracy.

Top ranking players attack the net not only behind a forcing drive shot, but also after almost every serve. Beginning and intermediate players should not follow this strategy unless their serve is strong and well controlled, otherwise a lot of needed energy will be wasted by coming in behind faults, and if the serves are shallow they will be sitters for easy passing returns. To be straightforward, you should come to the net behind a weak serve only to pick up the balls after a double fault. If, however, your serve has good though not necessarily overpowering speed, and if you can consistently place it deep, then rushing the net is worth a try, for it is a move that is mighty harassing to most opponents. Do not feel obligated to take the net behind *every* serve, but when you do advance you will need to go at it flat out, then pull up to a controlled hesitation just as your competitor is about to hit. Your charge should take you at least to within a few feet of the service line for your first volley. Finally, let your trip to the net be a natural continuation of the service stroke. The normal delivery already has you pressing forward, so as your back foot comes across the line to land in the court, make it the first step of your rush. Remember, though, that your initial task is to complete the serve. If you subconsciously begin your onslaught to the net *before* you send the ball on its way your serves will finish up in the screen behind the court.

The potential of the net game in singles is grossly underestimated by most players. An invasion of the net is always a torment for any opponent, but when your foe is an inexperienced player it often presents an agonizing plague that will beset him into making errors on routine balls. *In every match you play you should use the net game as part of your assault. Your very presence in the fore court may in itself be enough to press your opponent into defeating himself.*

It must not be concluded, however, that a net game is always a winning game. If you cannot volley at all, against a better opponent you may be better off playing most of the match from the relative security of the back court, for it takes more than aggressiveness to be able to employ an aggressive attack. Women players, often being less mobile than men, must of necessity plan their basic strategy around a back court game. Nevertheless, every player, in every match, must take advantage of at least the short ball to attack the net, if for no other reason than to keep your opponent from grooving himself to your base line game. Use the net less frequently if you are winning from the back court, but always use it. Keep it in reserve at the beginning of a match, for if you play it too often at the start it will eventually lose its surprise element, and if the match is a long one you may be too tired at the end to take the net at all. When your opponent can pass you well (and the only way to find that out is to try him), or when he has the knack of taking the ball on the rise, be more discreet with your trips to the fore court. If you are not hitting your smash well or you do not have confidence in it, let the ball bounce before you stroke it or simply punch out at the ball for a placement rather than a smash. If you do smash and your opponent gets his racket on the ball his return will always be a lob, and if your opponent habitually responds to your station at the net by throwing lobs over your head and then taking the net himself, a return lob will dislodge him again and often give you repossession of the fore court.

The net game is an exciting game. It adds spirit to the match and provides a unique challenge to both players. Even as a beginner it should be part of your planned strategy, for the percentage of winning a point from the net is very much in your favor. Play it within your capacities to play it well, but be open-minded enough to give it a go; you will find it to be the real fun part of tennis.

BASE LINE PLAY. For a player of tournament caliber, the main function of the base line game is to prepare the way for an attack on the net. By contrast, most weekend players consider a fairly permanent encampment on the base line to be the greatest guarantee of success. Regardless, for *all* players the base line game is a staple part of tennis. Without effective play in the back court a net rusher will have more difficulty making his advance, and a weekend player often is utterly lost.

Base line strategy can become surprisingly varied and complex, yet it can be broken down into some very fundamental principles. The most basic of these principles is almost anticlimactic in its simplicity: *to play the base line effectively you must be able to keep the ball in bounds.* Such a statement may not send Andy Capp to sobriety, but it does express the most elemental and hard-core truth of tennis. Weekend matches often set one base line player against another, and in such a case the contest becomes essentially one of ground stroke endurance, with the winner being the contestant who can best keep the ball in play.

Another of the fundamental principles is that *when playing from the base line you must learn to keep the ball deep.* Any shallow ball opens the door for your opponent to take the net. There are, of course, exceptions to this rule, but as a blanket strategy you must land your shots between your rival's service line and base line, the deeper the better. Playing the ball deep is not synonymous with hitting it hard. As long as your opponent remains back by his own base line, you should hit your ground shots to clear the top of the net by at least several feet. Do not allow the net to become an unnecessary barrier, but by the same token make sure you continue to stroke the ball instead of patting it across.

Next, you must expect that when playing from the base line a goodly percentage of your shots will be returned, and that your opponent will ordinarily be out to keep you on the run. In anticipation for the next play and to insure maximum court coverage, *between your shots you must return to a station on or just behind the base line at the center mark.* The pace of the game may not always allow you enough time to recover this basic position, but as long as you plan to continue your game from the back court you must make an attempt to return to that station after every shot.

The three most essential fundamentals, then, of the base line game are (1) the ball must be kept in play, (2) it must be kept deep, and (3) you must return to the basic base line position after every shot.

Beyond the three fundamental principles, the strategy of the base line game is contingent on the artifice of your opponent. Generally, you will be using your stronger strokes to attack his weaker ones, but the tactical employment of those strokes depends on whether your rival stays back near his own base line or frequently comes to the net. We will first consider how to deal with the more common of the two: the player who maintains a residence on the base line.

You will recall that as a net player you can ordinarily follow the simple strategy of attacking a ball to volley it beyond the reach of your opponent. However, when playing from the base line against a base line opponent, it is more difficult to pass him by. Instead, you must maneuver him around the court to either force him into an error or set him up for a winning placement. *Use the warm-up before the match (and the early part of the match) to judge the intensity of his returns. Some of his strokes may not come at you with the same vitality as others.* If there is a weaker side it usually is his backhand. Often a player will run around his left side to hit an off-balance forehand rather than risk a clean swipe with the backhand. *When your opponent shows you a weaker side, plan a liberal attack toward that side, but not to the point that he begins to groove his weak-side swing. You must also play into his strength to be able to exploit his weakness.* You can particularly afford to play his strong side when you have him on the run. Bear in mind, however, that in most cases the harder you hit to an opponent's strength the harder the ball will come back.

The first lesson in maneuvering your opposition is simply to run him alternately from side to side. By so doing it sets up a chance to fling a ball in back of him—to the area of the court he just left— which will either win the point outright or force him into a feeble return. Another tactic is to hold your opponent on one side of the court with several successive placements to that side, followed with a driving stroke to the opposite side. Often, as you repeat your placements to one flank, your rival will begin crowding that side, exposing an open area into which you can rifle your next shot. Those players who habitually run around their backhand are particularly susceptible to an assault which holds them on their backhand side followed by a placement to their forehand.

If your opponent has a favorite side, and if he becomes unnerved when he misses on several consecutive attempts from that side, it is often advantageous to attack his favorite side until he regains his confidence in it.

Many times a base line player will have full control of both the forehand and backhand, this being one of the probable reasons for his remaining in the back court. In this case running him from side to side may only result in well-placed cross-court returns which will pull you off the court. *Base line players who can hit equally well with both the forehand and backhand frequently employ a cross-court attack. If they are effective with their cross-court placements, running them from side to side will only facilitate their attack. In this circumstance it is better to play deep down-the-middle to them.* Such a plan not only lessens the cross-court advantage, but sometimes when a player who owns strong ground strokes is fed with a down-the-middle placement he is enticed by the chance to hit an outright winner and will press himself into an error because of overanxiousness.

If your opponent does not have particularly strong ground strokes, your own attack should be liberal with cross-court shots. They are safer attempts in that there is more area of the court to hit into and the ball usually crosses at the lowest point of the net. In addition, by hitting the ball early (out in front of your body) you can generate more racket head speed for a stronger shot. If you have trouble going cross-court with your backhand, go down-the-line or learn to lob with it. Your opponent often will have the same trouble, so expect a down-the-line or a lob return from off his backhand more frequently than from the forehand.

Finally, it should be recognized that a player who stays on the base line does so for a reason, and the reason usually is that he does not have confidence in his net game. Therefore, if you have the ability to chop the ball or drop it just over the net, then you have the most effective of all strategems, for you can bring the base liner to the area of the court he wants most to avoid. Then, having pulled him to the net, you can push him back again with a lob. Alternating these complementary shots (chop and lob) will tire your foe more quickly than chasing him along the base line. And, the spinning attack of the chop is harder to handle (as you know if you have played some table tennis). *Women players should especially learn to bring their opponents to the net. For some unexplained reason, very few girls seem to have a strong net game, and generally slower speed makes women players more vulnerable to the shallow shot.*

The chop attack is particularly effective against a hard hitter. It supplies you with the change of pace that is an absolute essential as a rebuttal for the player who can hit consistently well-placed, strong shots. If you cannot chop, a semi-lob will make a serviceable substitute, but make sure that you land the ball so that it bounces about shoulder high to your opponent where he cannot get his full and normal swing. Utilizing a change of pace strategy also requires that you be able to change from chops or semi-lobs back to a forcing flat attack.

If your opponent makes constant use of the chop and other spinning shots, bringing him to the net may be a less productive maneuver. Instead, keep him deep, for he probably has poor ground strokes. Send the ball low to him where he cannot chop it as well, and take the net often, for he probably will not be able to hit passing shots.

When you come up against a player who repeatedly advances to the net you must alter your strategy. *An opponent who frequently takes the net does so either because he is hiding a poor base line game or because he has confidence in his net play. To defeat him you must not allow him to use the offensive advantage of his position. Answer his charge to the net either with passing shots or with lobs.* Keep your passing shots low. Hit them firmly and with topspin if possible so that they will dip into the court after they have crossed the net. As a follow-up, anticipate that when you have hit a passing shot solidly but your opponent still manages to get his racket on the ball, his volley will be shallow and down-the-line. Finally, remember that the further away from the net you are when you make your passing attempt, the more time your opponent will have to move to his side to intercept the shot. Therefore, when hitting from deep in your own court, a lob may be a wiser choice. If you have difficulty hitting strong passing shots in the first place, your rival will win on your errors alone, and the lob again may be a more effective return. Hit your lobs just over the reach of the net player's racket. Keep them deep and generally to his backhand side where, if he catches up with the ball, he will be forced to hit a high backhand, the most diffiicult shot in all of tennis.

Make the net rusher consider the trip to the fore court a gamble. Whenever you can, force him to half-volley on his way in by pitching the ball at his feet, or, pour a few drives past him as he approaches, and soon he may lose his addiction for the net.

One final note: *when your opponent secures possession of the net, avoid the tendency to panic that is so common in many players. There is no need to take one eye off the ball to search out your rival's position, for you know exactly where he will be. Instead, invest your attention in the approaching ball and the shot you are about to make.*

The base line game is essentially a defensive game. As in most other sports, a defense is more durable and less subject to "off days" than an offense. However, a purely defensive game is also a dull game. Even if you rely largely on defense, steal a chance now and then to hit an outright winner, and take the net when the opportunity is given. You will find it more fun to win points with forcing shots than to have them handed to you via your opponent's mistakes.

STRATEGY AND THE SCORE.   When a match begins the point-by-point progress of the score will influence and vary the strategy of each game. It is imperative to know at all times what the tally is so that you can alter your plans accordingly. As a brief example of how your tactics might change as the score changes, let us "play through" what could well be a few typical games.

When your opponent is serving, play aggressively for the first two points, especially in the early games of the first set. If you win or share these two points, continue your aggressive play, but if you lose them the remainder of the game calls for a more conservative approach. Suppose your rival after the first two points has you down by a 30–love score. You can expect that he is now more likely to come to the net. As a counter for the anticipated net rush it is important to play away from his strength, hitting the ball to his weaker side or at his feet. Avoid by all means a shallow shot to his forehand, and keep the chop and drop shots for a time when the score is different. Assume now that you win the next point to make the score 30–15. The following point is a very crucial one, for it will give you either a deuce score or a deficit of 40–15 and only a meager chance at breaking service. Continue to keep the ball deep to your opponent's weaker side to reduce his opportunities for hitting a forcing stroke and crashing the net. If, however, you fall behind by a 40–15 count, you can anticipate that your enemy will take a crack at a "big" shot that will end the game. This is also the time for you to pull a few strings and chance an "impossible" shot for a point winner in the hope that if it is successful it will be a psychological boost for you and probably send your opponent back to a more conservative attack. Then, with

the score 40–30, the remainder of the game should be played at a
steady pace, taking no more chances.

In a game that you serve, hit your first attempts hard for the initial
two points. If you lose those two points to trail love–30, it is important
for you to get your first service attempt in for the next point, else your
opponent will attack your slower second service and probably take
the net. Send the serve to the far corner where it will pull your foe
off the court and make a net rush less likely, and, where there is more
room for you to make the serve good. Sometimes, when you are behind love–30 on your own service, if you play the ball continually
deep your opponent will be so anxious to break your service that he
will press himself into manufacturing his own mistakes.

In a more optimistic view, assume now that you win your first
two serves to lead 30–love. The next point is a most crucial one, for
if you win it to lead 40–love, you need to gain only one of the following three points to win the game, but if instead you lose the point to
run the score to 30–15, and then you win only one of the following
three points the score will be deuce. Leading 30–love on your own
service does not qualify for an attempt at a "big" shot hoping it will
go in. Hit your serve and other strokes firmly, but take no unnecessary
chances, for your rival will be playing conservatively and probably
will not approach the net. Only when you lead 40–love or perhaps
40–15 is a try for an "impossible" shot justified.

THE PRE-MATCH WARM-UP.   Tennis is one of the few sports in
the world in which opponents warm up against each other before the
start of the formal contest. This presents the players with the unique
opportunity of investigating each other's talents under a simulation
of the actual game. But far too many players fail to realize that this pre-
match rallying, usually called the hit-up, gives them a chance to or-
ganize their strategy before play begins. Instead they concentrate
all their attention on their own game and as a result they start the
match without a tactical plan. *By the time the match begins, all your
decisions should have already been made, and they must always be
based on the skills you have seen displayed by your opponent during
the hit-up.*

Use this pre-match time not only to groove your swing but also
to take an inventory of your rival. First of all judge his forehand and
backhand, and if you notice a weaker side do not play into it during
the hit-up. Give him some firm shots to see how he handles speed,
and fire a few right at his feet to discover whether he can take the
ball on the rise. Throw him some soft ones and note his response,
then prolong a rally to see if he becomes uneasy because of its length.
If you can, get him to the net to find out where he likes to place his
volley and how much confidence he has in his smash. Do not run him,
but do keep in mind that any errors he makes during the hit-up will
be magnified in the match. Make mental notes of all your observa-

tions, but after the match begins let your mind remain open to the possibility that you may have misread his talents in the hit-up.

Remember that, while you are making your pre-match observations of your opponent, he is probably doing the same of you. To keep him guessing, do not parade all your skills for his analysis, else he will have *your* game well discerned before the match begins.

Always use the warm-up for its original intent: to warm up! It is particularly important for you to hit at least a half-dozen serves into each court before you begin the contest, and especially when you are going to serve for the first game. The toss for the right of service should be made even before the hit-up so that each player can practice on the side of the court he will play for the first game. If your opponent wins the toss and elects to serve, and if the sun or wind is a factor on that particular day, make him serve into the sun and with the wind at his back. When the match begins hit aggressive service returns in that first game, for many players start the match so casually that they can easily have their service broken.

PLAY ON DIFFERENT COURT SURFACES. The bounce of a tennis ball from different court surfaces will vary somewhat according to the material used for the construction of the surface. Depending upon how the ball reacts from a bounce, a court is considered either slow or fast. Clay and composition are examples of slow courts, whereas grass, wood, cement and other hard surfaces are fast courts.

Clay courts require considerable maintenance and will dry slowly after a rain, but most players like the fact that clay is easier on the feet than hard-surface courts. Composition courts are a mixture of clay and pulverized brick or stone. They dry quickly following a rain, but have a tendency to become rough if they are not constantly maintained. The play of the ball from off these slower surfaces requires that the strategy of the game be altered from that employed on the more common hard-surface courts. The ball tends to "sit" after its bounce, consequently the players can catch up to it more easily and rallies are therefore longer. This reduces the advantage of a rush to the net since the opposing player will have more time to get into position to hit a strong return. When playing on a slow surface, take the net only when you are absolutely sure you have maneuvered your opponent into a position from which he cannot return a strong passing shot. Rarely follow your serve to the fore court. Try especially to get your first serves in, since an ace is less likely and therefore not worth the risk of error. From the base line, attempt a drive for an outright point winner less frequently than you would on a fast surface. Keep the ball alive, for on a slow court it is often the best defensive player who wins.

Hard-surface courts have the distinct advantage of being almost maintenance-free, therefore courts which receive heavy traffic (such as those at schools and colleges) are usually constructed with a surface

of cement, asphalt, or more commonly, one of the compounds manu-
factured especially for tennis court surfacing. Play on these courts is
faster and consequently there is an emphasis on the serve. Topspinning the serve is effective, since the ball will jump backward
from the bounce; a flat serve will skip off the court even more em-
phatically and usually force the receiver well behind the base line.

Wood courts are the fastest of all. Some school gymnasiums have
them, but otherwise they are quite uncommon. The one distinctive
feature of wood is the sure footing it affords. There is no tendency
to "skate" when coming to a quick stop.

Unless you someday reach the Wimbledon, U.S. Nationals, or
another top level tournament, you will probably never play on a
grass court. It may be just as well, for a grass court that is not expertly
manicured causes the ball to bounce so erratically that luck is a factor
in the outcome of a match.

There is some question as to which surface is the best for beginning players to learn on. Slow courts teach the player to place his shots
for accuracy and require that he learn a sound defensive game. However, it is probably better for you to have your first learning experiences on hard surface courts. The bounce of the ball is always true and
therefore allows you to develop confidence and a smooth swing more
quickly. In addition you can more readily adapt your game to a slow
court after having learned on a fast court than vice versa.

A SUMMARY OF STRATEGY.   The very first principle of winning
tennis is to keep your plan of strategy within your capabilities. Recognize your own strengths and weaknesses, and design your game
around the strengths. It is not necessary to master all the strokes to
win, but it is vital to know how to use the ones you have.

When a match begins, continue to stroke the ball as freely as you
do in practice; resorting to a pat-ball game demonstrates a lack of
confidence in your ability to keep the ball in-bounds. Even if you
start off the match by losing the first few games, do not change your
stroking style, for it often takes a few games to get your timing on
track.

Play against better opponents whenever you can, for you will
learn more by losing to a good player than you will by trouncing a
poor one. Try a more venturesome game against a better opponent—
your normal attack may never be good enough to win, but if you take
a few extra chances the ball may start falling in and give you the impetus to steal the match.

In every set, plan to beat your opponent six games to none. If
he wins one game, plan to beat him 6–1, and so on. Avoid the usual
tendency to relax when you have a sizeable lead, since it will always
be difficult to regain your original pace again if the score becomes
close.

Watch other players — the good ones to learn what to do and the poor ones to learn what not to do. Become a discriminating observer of tennis matches, watching the participants instead of the ball as most spectators will do. For a few games, keep your eyes on one player only. Observe his actions between strokes, for as in basketball, what you do without the ball is as important as what you do with the ball.

There is a well-worn saying that you should never change a winning game and always change a losing one. Some clarification of this philosophy is necessary, however. If you never change a winning game, you may find yourself playing monotonous tennis. Avoid stereotyping your game into a dull sameness. Try some new things, not necessarily revamping your entire game. If you are a base line player, use the net now and then, or hit an occasional spinning shot even though you lack real confidence in it. Take a few impossible chances in your matches, even if you get your fingers burned in the process. If an impossible shot falls good, do not feel absolutely confident that it will again the next time. If you are playing a losing game, do not panic yourself into making rash alterations. If change is called for, have the flexibility to change, but give your strategy the fair trial of perhaps as much as the first set of a match before you make any serious adjustments. The important thing is to know exactly why the points are going against you.

When wind affects the flight of the ball, hit more firmly and lob more frequently when it is in your face (hit the lobs deeper than normal). When the wind is at your back play steady tennis; try for placements rather than outright winners, hit with topspin if you can, and take the net often. Topspin your serves to keep them from picking up the wind and sailing out of the service court. If the wind is cross-court, angle your shots toward it.

When playing against a left-handed opponent, remember that the ball will break opposite to a right-hander. If he hits a topspin serve that is especially bothersome, move up on the ball to take it early and give the spin less time to work its effect. If you are a lefty, learn to spin your serve and ground strokes to get the full advantage of the hazard it presents to your opponents.

When the balls you are using in a match are worn, hit your strokes flat (without spin) and try especially for placements, but when the balls are new they will respond well to a spinning game, especially on the serve.

If you fall into one of those horrendous spells when the net seems higher on your side and the court shorter on the other side, it may be wise to avoid competitive tennis for a while and return to the practice courts, or avoid all tennis for a week or so. Sometimes this lay-off will be in itself just the medicine your game needed.

THE DOUBLES GAME

Anyone who has ever played tennis doubles would doubtlessly agree that the game is an interesting and unique diversity from singles. Perhaps it was the original game, for no one is quite certain whether tennis began as a sport for two, four, or even more players. Wimbledon held the world's first doubles tournament in 1879, just two years after originating the singles tournament, and since that time the game has grown to be universally appealing to all people.

In the doubles game there are twice as many players on the court, often resulting in twice as much confusion, for doubles teams seldom set down any pre-match planning. For this reason partners who have taken stock of their abilities and analyzed the game itself frequently can defeat better opponents who have given less attention to their strategy. Most of this lack of planning is a matter of circumstance, since doubles matches are usually "pickup" matches. With the exclusion of tournament play, partners are likely to be different from one match to the next, and as a result the two players are not familiar enough with each other's style and lack time to formulate a joint strategy. With this in mind our discussion of doubles tactics here will be briefer than that of the singles game, and will be oriented toward those tactics which each player can utilize individually without being familiar with his partner's skills. For a more comprehensive analysis of doubles strategy the reader is advised to consult Bill Talbert's *The Game of Doubles in Tennis,* easily the finest book ever written on the subject.

The tactical plan of doubles is based on the very nature of the game. Since there are two players covering the court, driving shots are less frequent than in singles. The serve, volley and smash are the offensive weapons, with the lob as the principal defensive stroke. The overwhelming strategic objective of doubles play is to gain and hold possession of the net, for the team that owns the net will win the match. To this end the serving team starts each point with one partner already stationed at the net, and the server will follow his serves to the fore court, while the receiving team must plan for frequent use of the lob to dislodge the serving team from their position and take the net themselves. Excluding the service and the return of the service, some 80 per cent of points in better play are scored from the fore court, and about 80 per cent of those points are scored from a volley.

THE SERVICE. Like tactical warfare, the game of doubles is based on positioning. In this respect the serving team has an advantage over the receiving team since the partner of the server is already at the net at the start of each point. From this net position he is responsible for guarding the alley, but he can also move toward center court to intercept a feeble return. *His distance from the net is generally six to eight feet,* but is dependent on his height and his ability to react quickly. He is across the net from the service court into which the serve is to be made, and about three feet inside the *singles* side line. The net player must avoid the tendency to unknowingly drift toward the center of the court during an exchange of shots, thus exposing his alley, and he must resist creeping too close to the net where he will invite a lob.

The server takes his position midway between the center mark and the singles side line, regardless of which court he is serving into, and his net charge is straight forward from that station.

These are the conventional positions for the server and his partner. They allow for maximum court coverage and are to be suggested for the great majority of doubles teams. However, under certain circumstances, alterations may be tried. If, for example, the server has a very weak backhand, the net man may want to maintain a position always to the left of the center line to prevent the opponents from continually driving into the server's backhand. As a psychological hazard to the opponents, the serving team could use the tandem formation (often called the Australian formation) where the net man is always on the same side of the center line as the server. This positioning reduces the opponents' opportunities for cross-court returns, but dangerously exposes the backhand of both players when the serve is made to the deuce court.

The server must almost without exception always hit a topspin serve. The reasons for this are twofold. First, it allows him more time to move into the fore court (unless the serve is very weak, *all* players, including women, should follow their serves to the fore court), and second, *the server must make his first serve good,* therefore the topspin should be used since it is more easily controlled. If the server constantly faults on his first attempts, he will waste needed energy in coming to the net behind those faults, and the receiver will be able to move up on the court where he can make a more effective placement on the service return, thus nullifying the positional advantage of the server's partner.

Generally all serves must be hit deep to the receiver's backhand corner for the weaker return it will induce. Hitting to the backhand in the deuce court has the added advantage of depriving the receiver of his down-the-alley return possibilities, and a serve to the backhand in the advantage court will pull the receiver off the court to open up a wide area in the middle of the court for placing the volley. Of course, an occasional serve to the forehand corner keeps everything honest, and an occasional flat serve (but only a rare occasion) keeps the receivers from priming themselves for the topspin.

THE RETURN OF THE SERVICE. The service return is the most important shot in doubles. While a service break-through is more difficult than in the singles game, if the receivers can return the ball they may be able to wrest the net from the serving team and switch the odds on winning the point.

Since the server stands further away from the center mark than in singles, *the receiver will generally take up a station just inside the singles side line, and he must be in as far as his ability to take the ball on the rise will allow.* Every step he can be in will mean less time for the server to charge the net. Men should try to and women should almost always receive from inside the base line.

The receiver's talents largely determine the station taken up by the receiver's partner. If the receiver has a difficult time returning the serves, his partner should be just inside the base line and near the singles side line. If the receiver can return the serves with some consistency, his partner should be half-way between the base line and the service line, and a few feet inside the singles side line. From this position both players can either charge the net or retreat together, depending on the circumstances. It is the most common station for the receiver's partner, and is to be recommended for most weekend male players and for all women. Finally, if the receiver can continually hit firm service returns, his partner should be a step inside the service line and half-way between the center line and the singles side line. This formation is called the modified net position and has been successfully used by Australian doubles teams since the early 1900's.

How you arrange yourselves to receive the serve depends on the stroking abilities of both players. Keep in mind that the rules require each player to receive in the same court throughout the set, therefore the partner with the weaker backhand should receive in the deuce court.

Several options are available for placement of the return. *The first choice is to hit it back to the feet of the server, forcing him to volley up.* The next preference is a lob over the net man. This is an especially good return from the deuce court, since it will force the server to hit a high backhand. A further possibility is a passing drive hit to the outside of the net man, but this down-the-alley shot can be executed only on serves that come to the far corner in either service court. A less frequent attempt would be a hard shot right at the net man (preferably to his right side where he will have more difficulty getting the racket into position). Sometimes a net man will be so anxious to get his racket on any ball that comes his way that he will err on balls which would have gone out had he let them go. Short chops and other dink-type shots should be used only when they can be well controlled, for a poor dink shot is either a sitter or an invitation to the net. Finally, a firm shot can be made between the serving partners or cross-court beyond the server's reach.

FORE COURT PLAY. Any doubles team that plays a base line game can win points only on the mistakes of their opponents. The

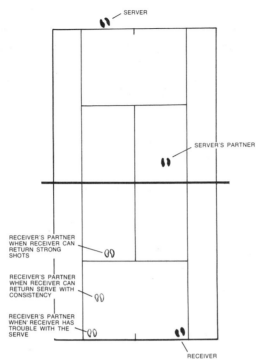

SERVER

SERVER'S PARTNER

RECEIVER'S PARTNER
WHEN RECEIVER CAN
RETURN STRONG
SHOTS

RECEIVER'S PARTNER
WHEN RECEIVER CAN
RETURN SERVE WITH
CONSISTENCY

RECEIVER'S PARTNER
WHEN RECEIVER HAS
TROUBLE WITH THE
SERVE

RECEIVER

Conventional positions
of serving and receiving
team in doubles.

total strategy of the doubles game, for both the serving and receiving team, must be aimed essentially at gaining a stronghold on the net.

In his charge of the net, the server must expect that the receiver's return will come his way. Since the server will, at this time, only have reached a position just behind the service line, *he must play his first volley deep (and ordinarily down-the-middle)* to enable him to finish off his charge to the net.

The receiver's best opportunities for stealing the net from the serving team will come off a low, cross-court return of the serve, or more frequently, by employing the lob. *When a team playing the base line lobs over a team playing the net they should always follow that lob to the fore court. The lob should be hit either to the backhand corner or up the middle where it may cause indecision between the two partners as to who will return the shot.* Often, when a team is dislodged from its net position by a lob, the best strategy for that team is to answer with a lob of their own.

As in singles, overanxious players who station themselves too close to the net will encourage a lob from their opponents. *The basic position for both partners is six to eight feet from the net and midway between the singles side line and the center line (each partner, of course, in his own half of the court).* When it appears that the opponents are about to lob, both partners should move back a step or two in anticipation for the shot. And when the net team has made a forcing shot that is retrieved by the opponents behind their own base line, they should move up a step or two in anticipation for their coming volley.

Ordinarily, the smash should be hit at the feet of one of the opponents, or cross-court when the opportunity is available for a sharply angled shot. The best area for placement of the volley can be answered by a well-known baseball phrase made by a player who, when asked how he managed to keep his batting average so high, responded by saying, "It's easy. I just hit the ball where they ain't!"

When one of the net players must move to the side or off the court to retrieve a ball, his partner should also move toward that side to maintain maximum court coverage. And, when a lob is made over the head of one player, *both* partners should retreat from the net, for *the side-by-side formation must constantly be maintained during a rally.*

A drive hit between the net players should be taken by the partner who can receive the ball with a forehand, and when a lob is hit up-the-middle over the heads of the net team, it should again be taken by the partner who can hit a forehand return. Sometimes, however, when a lob is hit over one player, it is the other player who will have the best chance to retrieve the shot. In a case where this happens, *the two players will switch sides of the court and then continue on those sides until the completion of the point (this scissors-like switching is also necessary when a serve is returned over the head of the net man).*

POACHING AND DRIFTING.   A poach is a natural happening in the course of play in which one player will move into his partner's half of the court to retrieve a ball. Drifting occurs when one player anticipates where the opponent's next shot will come, and then moves toward that spot before the ball is on its way. Often a net man will drift toward center court during the serve to cut off the expected cross-court return. The danger in this move is, of course, that it opens the alley. Drifting and poaching will almost always happen when one player is at the net and the other is at the base line, and when it does happen the player who is not retrieving the ball must move into a position that allows the team to assure full court coverage. Again, it is to be emphasized that during play after the serve and the return of the serve, the doubles team must maintain a side-by-side position, for when one man is at the net and the other back, the net man will often be unaware of his partner's position and will drift or poach for a ball that should have been left for his partner. In these cases, the team often leaves one whole side of their court vacant.

BASE LINE PLAY.   The entire plan of the base line game is to prepare the way for an attack on the net. As already indicated, this is best accomplished by use of the lob or a low, cross-court service return. However, when the opposing team is at the net, a sharply hit drive placed between the net partners will often result in an outright point winner since it causes confusion between them as to who will take the ball. Or a sizzling drive hit right at one of the net players will frequently result in a point by virtue of its speed alone.

When a base line player is forced off the side of the court to retrieve a ball, the return should always be down-the-line. And, in anticipation of such a return, the net team should drift toward the side of court the ball is on.

Mixed Doubles

While tennis is already a friendly game, it becomes even friendlier when the company is mixed. Winning is relegated to a subordinate role, and the game takes on a lighter atmosphere.

Men should recognize that it is customary for them to serve first at the start of a set, but that it is courteous to ask a female partner if she would like to be the first server instead. Generally, when serving to a woman, a man should ease up on the speed of his serves, but not to the point that he is patting the ball. Usually, he should receive the serve in the backhand (left) court, and during a rally he should not hit incessantly to the female opponent to win the point.

Mixed doubles teams should play in the side-by-side formation and poaching or drifting should be done infrequently. When a ball comes between the partners, it is generally the man who will take the shot, unless the woman can handle it. All "sitters" for a smash belong to the man (again, unless the woman can more easily take it), and the smash is rarely hit toward the female opponent.

PRACTICE

Any tennis player who is serious enough about his game to want to improve it should occasionally go to the courts with the sole intent of practicing. If you have a desire to become skilled, then you must have a willingness to work at it, but the tensions of actual match competition do not always create the best learning situations. Frequently, the conditions of the match will ingrain errors rather than repair them. The remedy instead may be to devote a few sessions to practice only, with no match play included. Furthermore, it is important to know what to do during these sessions to gain the greatest benefit from them. In this respect, a few suggestions for practice follow.

Practice hints

First, practice only with someone who is also interested in rehearsing his own strokes. If you go to the court for practice, then do just that, not letting your friend talk you into a match five minutes after your session begins.

If you are in a hitting slump, you will probably also be in a state of discouragement, so try especially to relax during practice. Return your thoughts to the basic fundamentals of the game, looking first at your grip, then checking your pivot and backswing, making sure you are bringing the racket back early enough. Give some attention to a free follow-through, for an abbreviated swing is a sign of tension.

Start the practice session by hitting long ground strokes, both you and your friend stroking the ball from behind the base line. Hit everything you can get your racket on, even if the ball comes to you out-of-bounds, and do not get in the habit of letting the ball bounce a second time before hitting it as so many players do in practice. You cannot do it in a match, so avoid doing it in practice. Before you start the session, be prepared to run several miles, then go after every ball just as you would in a match.

During this period of long hitting women especially need to pay attention to keeping their grip firm and the racket face flat at contact (women players have a tendency to incline the face of the racket when hitting long strokes). Remember that in the ladies' game this base line attack is more common than among the men, so it is important to groove your ground strokes.

Keep up the long hitting until it gets dull, then switch to something else. Exaggerate the use of your weak points, perhaps requesting your friend to feed you a certain type of shot so you can concentrate on a weak stroke. Only practice one thing at a time, though.

Do not be a stroke purist during these sessions. Individualize somewhat and try new things. If you never have before, experiment with spinning the ball, especially if you are female, since it is so much more lethal in the ladies' game. If you have strong wrists, try incorporating a bit of a wrist snap in your strokes, even though it's against all principles (except in the serve and smash). Lew Hoad and Rod Laver have shown the tennis world that "wristy" shots can indeed be used effectively for deceptive placement of the ball, so give it a try in practice.

Anticipation can only be learned, and the practice sessions are the place to learn it. Try to "sense" where the next ball will come, and set yourself to move toward that spot. Recognize that the direction a player is going to hit the ball is usually given away by where he places his foot as he steps into the ball, that is, when he steps across his body for a forehand drive he will usually hit to his right, and when he steps to his left he will usually hit in that direction.

Most tennis courts have a practice wall or a backboard. When hitting against it, make sure you return to the ready position between your strokes. The ball comes off the wall in a hurry, and for this reason it is effective in teaching you to get the racket in early preparation for the stroke.

Avoid cluttering your mind with all kinds of finical details of the strokes in practice. Often, thinking of a lot of the details will interrupt the rhythm of the swing. Roy Emerson once said that he "couldn't think and play tennis at the same time," meaning that he had practiced every stroke for so long that he had developed instinctive movements in the game. As any good player, he had conditioned himself to the circumstances of the strokes so that in a match he could put his mind to his strategy rather than the mechanics of his strokes. With experience and plenty of practice, your strokes will also become instinctive. Practice is the very basis of the game, and for this reason each session should be taken seriously as a time to discipline your swing so that in the next match you play your mind will be less on your strokes and more on your tactics.

Glossary

Ace – A point winning serve that is hit beyond the reach of the receiver.

Advantage – The next point after a deuce score. The player who wins the point is said to have the "advantage," and if he also wins the following point he has won the game; if not the score returns to deuce. Often abbreviated to "ad," a score of "ad in" means the advantage belongs to the server, while "ad out" refers to the receiver's advantage.

Approach shot – A ground stroke hit by a player on his way to the net.

Back court – The area around the base line.

Backhand – A stroke used to play a ball on the left side of a right-handed player, and vice versa.

Backspin – Backward spin on the ball; that is, with the top of the ball rotating away from the direction of its flight.

Base line game – A manner of play in which the player remains near his own base line and advances only infrequently to the fore court.

Change of pace – The strategy of varying the speed of the ball from stroke to stroke.

Chop – A stroke in which the racket is brought into the ball while moving downward as well as forward, imparting backspin to the ball.

Cross-court shot – Hitting the ball from one side of the court across the net to the side diagonally opposite.

Davis Cup – A series of men's team matches from different nations, played in elimination-type tournament for several months each year, with the final matches in December.

Deuce – An even score after six or more points of a game have been played. When referring to games it is an even score in games after ten or more have been played.

Dink – A term referring to any softly hit shot, sometimes with a great deal of spin, but usually intended to keep the ball in play rather than to be an outright point winner.

Double fault – Failure of a player to get either of his two service attempts into the proper service court.

Doubles – Match play between two teams of two players each. In mixed doubles a man and a woman play as partners on each team.

Down-the-line shot – A ball hit across the net parallel to a side line.

Drive – A firm forehand or backhand shot hit from a full swing, intended to be either an outright point winner or to force a weak return from the opponent.

Drop shot – A ball hit softly, usually with backspin, so that it just clears the net and lands very close to it.

Fault – A served ball that does not land within the proper service court.

105

Foot fault—A service delivery that is illegal, usually because the server steps on the base line or into the court before his racket contacts the ball.

Forehand—A stroke used to play a ball on the right side of a right-handed player, or the left side of a left-handed player.

Game—A unit of a set completed when one side wins four points before the other side wins three. When both sides have scored at least three points, the winner of the game is the first side to gain a two point lead.

Ground stroke—A forehand or backhand stroke used to hit a ball after it has bounced.

Half-volley—A "pick-up" stroke, usually defensive, in which the ball is contacted just as it begins to rise from a bounce.

Hold service—A term used when a game is won by the server.

ILTF—The International Lawn Tennis Federation; the organization that governs tennis throughout the world.

Let—Any point that must be replayed. Most often, a ball that hits the top of the net from a serve, then lands in the proper service court.

Lob—A high, arching shot that lands near the opponent's base line.

Love—A score of zero. In a love game one side wins no points; in a love set one side wins no games.

Match—A contest between two or four players in which one side must win a predetermined number of games or sets to be declared the winner.

Match point—Term used when a side needs but one more point to win the match.

Net game—A manner of play in which a player frequently advances to the fore court to use the volley and smash.

Overhead or *smash*—A free-swinging stroke used for a ball that is over a player's head. Its motion closely resembles the serve.

Passing shot—To send the ball across the net to either side of an opponent beyond his reach.

Poach—Applies usually to the net man in doubles when he leaves his half of the court to intercept a ball in his partner's territory.

Rally—The exchange of shots between opponents after the service, usually referring to prolonged play.

Serve—The stroke used to put the ball into play at the start of each point. The more inclusive term *service* applies to the right to be the server and to the served ball itself.

Service break—Term used when a game is won by the receiver rather than the server.

Set—A unit of a match completed when one side wins six games, or when one side gains a lead of two games after both sides have won at least five games.

Set point—Term used when a side needs but one more point to win the set.

Singles—Match play between two players.

Tie-breaker—A scoring system designed to eliminate prolonged sets. If any set becomes tied at 6 games each, players may elect to play either a 5-of-9 or a 7-of-12 point tie-breaking game.

Topspin—Forward spin on the ball; that is, with the top of the ball rotating in the direction of its flight.

USLTA—The United States Lawn Tennis Association; the organization that governs tennis in America.

VASSS—The Van Alen Simplified Scoring System. There are several types, one of which is the "no-ad," in which, with a score of 40-all, the next point wins the game.

Volley—A short punch stroke used to hit the ball before it bounces.

Wightman Cup—An annual competition between women players representing Great Britain and the United States.

Bibliography

Danzig, Allison, and Peter Schwed (ed.). *The Fireside Book of Tennis.* New York, Simon and Schuster, 1972. The most complete history of the game and its great players ever published. Includes eye-witness reporting of the all-time great matches, and a how-to-play section written by expert players. A massive, intriguing spectrum of the entire game of tennis.

Fisk, Loring. *How to Beat Better Tennis Players.* Garden City, N. J., Doubleday and Company, Inc., 1970. A very comprehensive treatment of the strategy of tennis play. Presented in situational format. It covers every conceivable aspect of play, including how women should play against a male opponent.

King, Billie Jean. *Tennis to Win.* New York, Harper and Row, 1970. Fairly typical in its instructional material, but it is an interesting narrative by the most controversial of women players. Includes an excellent section on strategy.

Laver, Rod. *How to Play Championship Tennis.* New York, Macmillan Company, 1965. The story of Laver himself; how he grew up with tennis and the things he learned along the way. The writing is delightfully flamboyant and is interspersed with techniques of play that are explained without the burden of trite details. While not truly an instructional text, the instruction it gives is remarkably succinct and meaningful.

Murphy, Bill, and Chet Murphy. *Tennis for Beginners.* New York, Ronald Press Company, 1958. One of the few books written especially for youngsters, it makes use of a "buddy system" by which two beginning tennis players can help each other in acquiring skills.

Ramo, Simon. *Extraordinary Tennis for the Ordinary Player.* New York, Crown Publishing Company, 1970. A very witty, even funny analysis of the typical weekend player. Remarkably light and fascinating reading, and its whimsical style includes surprisingly succinct skill and strategic applications for all recreational players.

Talbert, William F., and Bruce S. Old. *The Game of Doubles in Tennis.* Philadelphia, J. B. Lippincott Company, 1956. Easily the most comprehensive treatise ever written on the doubles game, this text cannot be read over lightly; it must be studied. The tactics it presents are sometimes complicated, but those players who are serious about their doubles game will find it most intriguing.

Talbert, William F., and Bruce S. Old. *The Game of Singles in Tennis.* Philadelphia, J. B. Lippincott Company, 1962. The techniques of singles play are presented in a down-to-earth fashion and are supported by statistics compiled in championship matches. For the strategist, this book is a must. Even beginners will be able to employ the suggested tactics.

Talbert, William F., and Bruce S. Old. *Stroke Production in the Game of Tennis.* New York, J. B. Lippincott Company, 1971. Lucid guide to the correct execution of the basic strokes in tennis, with plenty of illustrations and personified descriptions of the techniques of better players.

Tennis. 297 Westport Ave., Norwalk, Conn. 06856. A monthly periodical that includes more instructional articles than any other magazine of tennis. Excellent reading for players with some experience.

Tennis Times. 3000 France Ave. So., Minneapolis, Minn. 55416. Quarterly magazine published first for the fan and second for the player. Insights into various aspects of tennis beyond the courts.

Trabert, Tony. *Winning Tennis for Weekend Players.* New York, Holt, Reinhart, and Winston, 1972. A guide to the doubles game for occasional players. Practical, applicable, presented in question and answer form, and beneficial for all doubles teams.

World Tennis Magazine. Box 3, Gracie Station, New York, N. Y. 10028. The finest of tennis periodicals, it presents generally advanced instructional articles along with features about players, tournaments and so on. Reading it is the best way to keep up-to-date in the tennis world.